30

SEASONS AT

WHITE HART LANE

1974-75 TO 2003-04

David Powter

SOCCER BOOKS LIMITED

CONTENTS

British Library Cataloguing in Publication Data
A catalogue record for this book is available from the British Library

ISBN 1-86223-095-1

Copyright © 2004, SOCCER BOOKS LIMITED (01472 696226)
72 St. Peter's Avenue, Cleethorpes, N.E. Lincolnshire, DN35 8HU, England
Web site   www.soccer-books.co.uk
e-mail   info@soccer-books.co.uk

Printed by 4edge Ltd. www.4edge.co.uk

TOTTENHAM HOTSPUR – 30 SEASONS 1974-1975 TO 2003-2004

INTRODUCTION

Founded in 1882, Tottenham Hotspur is one of the most famous clubs in English football. All-told the club has won 16 major trophies (two League titles and 14 cups) and five of these were lifted during the 30 years up to the summer of 2004.

Spurs fans enjoyed three successive campaigns of UEFA Cup football during the early 1970s. Bill Nicholson's side triumphed in 1971-72, defeating Wolverhampton Wanderers in an all-English Final. It was the North London club's second success in Europe, having defeated Atletico Madrid in the 1962-63 European Cup Winners' Cup Final, in Rotterdam.

The holders of the UEFA Cup reached the semi-final stage again in 1972-73, where they met Liverpool. Spurs went down 1-0 to Bill Shankly's side in the first leg at Anfield; but fought back magnificently in the home leg. They gained victory on the night, by a 2-1 scoreline, but slipped out of the competition on away goals. However, despite their disappointment, the Spurs faithful left White Hart Lane that night safe in the knowledge that their side would soon have another crack at the UEFA Cup, qualification coming through their success in the League Cup. Ironically, both Liverpool and Wolves were side-stepped en route to a Final meeting with Norwich City.

Tottenham Hotspur became the first club to win the League Cup twice (having also won it two years earlier), with substitute Ralph Coates' second half strike proving to be the only goal of that dreary 1972-73 Final.

The 1973-74 UEFA Cup campaign was another lengthy one. Nicholson's side defeated Grasshoppers, Aberdeen, Dynamo Tbilisi, Cologne and Lokomotive Leipzig to earn two matches with Feyenoord in the Final. Four goals were shared in London; but it was the Dutch side who triumphed 2-0 in a not so memorable night in Rotterdam.

Spurs completed their 1973-74 Division One fixtures in 11th place, following finishes of eighth, sixth and third, respectively, in the previous three seasons. Those lengthy cup runs could not paper over the cracks of a decline.

1974-1975 SEASON

Tottenham made a disastrous start to the campaign, losing their first four League fixtures. Three games were lost 1-0. Ipswich Town won at White Hart Lane, while trips to Manchester City and newly promoted Carlisle United proved equally fruitless.

Martin Peters netted Spurs' first goal of 1974-75, in match four, but it was Manchester City who triumphed 2-1 to secure an early 'double' over the North Londoners.

Despair down Tottenham High Road quickly turned to shock when Bill Nicholson announced his resignation after nearly 16 years at the helm. The much-liked Yorkshireman had guided Spurs to eight major trophies. In 1960-61 he became the first manager in the 20th century to lead a team to the League and Cup 'Double'.

The board and the players tried to persuade the disillusioned manager to change his mind. But it was all to no avail and a successor was sought. The board's choice was a surprise one in the form of Hull City boss Terry Neill. The Northern Irishman had shown managerial promise with the Tigers, but his best days as a player had been with Tottenham's nearest and most hated rivals Arsenal.

Neill was given a five-year contract and immediately gave up his role as manager of Northern Ireland. He quickly made it clear that he wanted to run things his own way. He said "I admire Bill Nicholson, but I am my own man." The new era got off to a promising start with a home victory over West Ham United, followed by another success at Wolverhampton. However, they were soon stuttering again and only one of the next eight fixtures ended in triumph. That one win was a memorable one, however, with Steve Perryman and Martin Chivers on target as Arsenal were beaten 2-0 at White Hart Lane.

Tottenham climbed to 15th place, their highest position of the season, on 7th December when they defeated Newcastle United 3-0 at home. However, it proved to be somewhat of a false dawn and only one of the next 14 games ended in victory. That match was the return encounter with the Magpies at St James' Park. Neill's side romped to a 4-0 half-time lead and eventually won 5-2, with Alfie Conn bagging Tottenham's only hat-trick of 1974-75.

Spurs were in dire danger of being relegated, lying in 20th place, with just seven fixtures to be be fulfilled. Victories over Wolves and Queen's Park Rangers on successive days eased the pressure, but even after two more wins (and two defeats) they were sat in 21st place staring at the precipice. The official 'last' day of the season had been and gone, but Spurs still had a re-arranged home game with Leeds United to fulfil. A point would have been enough to earn safety but the bulk of the 43,752 crowd went home deliriously happy after watching a 4-2 win. Cyril Knowles netted twice as Spurs finished 19th, just one point above both Luton Town and Chelsea (with Carlisle United also relegated).

Former Dundee striker John Duncan netted in four consecutive games during the run-in to finish top scorer with 12 goals. Chivers contributed ten goals; but no other player scored more than six times, with Spurs only netting 52 goals during the season.

Tottenham experienced no joy in the cups in 1974-75. They lost 4-0 at home to Middlesbrough in the second round of the League Cup and slipped to a 1-0 home defeat against Second Division Nottingham Forest in an F.A. Cup third round replay.

Among the men wearing a Tottenham shirt for the last time in 1974-75 were Phil Beal (333 League games – 1 goal), Welsh international Mike England (299 – 14) and the Norwich-bound World Cup winner Peters (189 – 46).

BILL NICHOLSON

Reign: 1958-1974

Honours: European Cup Winners' Cup, UEFA Cup, Football League, F.A. Cup (3 times) and the League Cup

Highest League finish: Champions in 1960-61

Best F.A. Cup Run: Winners in 1960-61, 1961-62 and 1966-67

Best League Cup Run: Winners in 1970-71 and 1972-73

Best European Run: European Cup Winners' Cup Winners in 1962-63 and UEFA Cup Winners in 1970-71

1975-1976 SEASON

An opening day victory over Middlesbrough seemed to suggest that Spurs would experience better times in 1975-76. However, that turned out to be the club's only League win of the first 12 matches. Seven of those early season games ended all-square, including the home fixture with Norwich, when Glenn Hoddle came off the bench to make his League debut.

Successive wins over Leicester City and Wolves propelled Neill's side towards the middle of the table and that was basically where they remained until they enjoyed an end-of-season purple patch. Four successive victories took them up to a seasonal peak of sixth place. However, only one of last four matches ended in victory and they had to be content with finishing in ninth place.

Experienced full-backs, Joe Kinnear (196 League games – 2 goals) and Cyril Knowles (401 – 14) wore Tottenham shirts for the last time during the first half of the season. Martin Chivers (278 – 118) also departed, in the summer of 1976, to join Swiss side Servette Geneva. Chivers was the third highest scorer in 1975-76, behind the Johns – Duncan and Pratt – who netted 20 and 10 times respectively. Duncan was the Division's second top scorer.

Spurs were knocked out of the F.A. Cup by Stoke City in a third round replay; but did register five victories in the League Cup. Doncaster Rovers were defeated 7-2 at White Hart Lane in the quarter-final and Newcastle United were beaten 1-0 in the first leg of the semi-final. Sadly, the chance of another visit to Wembley Stadium disappeared when the Magpies won the return at St James' Park 3-1, with the help of a hotly disputed opening goal.

TERRY NEILL

Reign: 1974-1976
Honours: None
Highest League finish: 9th in 1975-76
Best F.A. Cup Run: Round 3 in 1974-75 and 1975-76
Best League Cup Run: Semi-final in 1975-76

1976-1977 SEASON

Terry Neill resigned during the summer of 1976 to become Bertie Mee's successor at Arsenal. Assistant-manager Wilf Dixon followed his old boss to Highbury. The Tottenham board asked coach Keith Burkinshaw to be the new manager.

Burkinshaw's side got off to an insipid start, collecting just one point from three games. However, their first League victory came at Old Trafford and was quickly followed by a home win over Leeds United.

Spurs struggled to find the net in 1976-77 and, with only five wins during the first half of the season, it became increasingly obvious that they would be involved in the relegation dog-fight. Back-to-back successes over Norwich and Liverpool bred hope down Tottenham High Road; but Burkinshaw's squad (although boosted by the arrival of winger Peter Taylor) was not strong enough to survive. A 5-0 defeat at Maine Road sealed their fate and, in spite of a last match win over Leicester City, Spurs finished bottom (in 22nd place) with 33 points. They finished one point behind also relegated Stoke City and Sunderland, and two points behind the 'safe' pair of Coventry City and Bristol City.

Chris Jones was Tottenham's top scorer with nine goals. That was one more than Taylor and two more than the penalty-taker Keith Osgood. Spurs only scored 48 League goals, but the defence won few plaudits either, conceding 72 goals. They let in four of more goals on five occasions, their worst defeat being the 8-2 humiliation at Derby.

There was to be little joy in the cups, with Welsh sides knocking them out in the third round of both domestic competitions. Third Division Wrexham triumphed at White Hart Lane in the League Cup, while second-flight Cardiff City halted their F.A. Cup campaign at Ninian Park.

1977-1978 SEASON

After 27 seasons in the top-flight, Tottenham Hotspur kicked off 1977-78 in the Second Division. The board kept faith with Keith Burkinshaw, a decision that was to reap dividends with their First Division status regained at the first attempt.

Barry Daines inherited the number one jersey after Pat Jennings was allowed to join Terry Neill at Highbury – after making 472 League appearances for Tottenham. Burkinshaw's side were never out of the top three and threatened to run away with the championship during an unbeaten 19-match run which took them to the top of the table. Bristol Rovers received the biggest hiding when they were slaughtered 9-0 at White Hart Lane, in October, with Colin Lee netting four times and Ian Moores grabbing a hat-trick.

The only defeats in the first 36 League fixtures came at Hull and Bolton. However, promotion was nearly thrown away with three matches lost during the run-in, including a home reverse against Sunderland. In the end a victory over Hull City and a goalless draw at the Dell proved just enough to secure the third promotion place. It was a close call though, with Spurs registering 56 points, the same as Brighton. The Seagulls had the inferior goal difference and stayed down in fourth place. Only two points split the top four places with champions Bolton finishing on 58 points, one in front of Southampton.

For the third time in four seasons 16-goal Duncan headed the club's list of goalscorers. Glenn Hoddle bagged 12 goals, while Lee and Peter Taylor netted 11 goals apiece. Burkinshaw was lucky to have a settled squad, with Daines, skipper Steve Perryman, Neil NcNab, John Pratt, Terry Naylor, Taylor and Hoddle missing only 11 games between them. The first four named players being ever-present.

Tottenham slipped out of both cups at the third round stage. Coventry ended their League Cup ambitions at White Hart Lane, while Bolton triumphed in an F.A. Cup third round replay at Burnden Park, after extra-time.

1978-1979 SEASON

The 1978-79 campaign not only saw Tottenham back in the top-flight, but also saw the surprise arrival in London N17 of two of the Argentinian squad that had won the World Cup only a few weeks earlier. It was a massive coup by Keith Burkinshaw and the recruitment of Ossie Ardiles and Ricky Villa was eventually to pay off in terms of silverware. However, the initial road was rocky with Spurs enjoying a mixed return to the First Division. They were hammered 7-0 at Anfield, in early September, but responded by winning four of their next six fixtures to climb to eighth place in the table.

Spurs spent most of the season in the top half, but a ten match winless run in the spring spun them down to 16th place. Victories in the last two matches (at Bolton and at home to West Bromwich Albion) enabled Burkinshaw's side to finish in a creditable 11th place. Peter Taylor netted 11 times to finish as the top scorer, while Colin Lee and Glenn Hoddle were both on target seven times.

Third Division Swansea City were too good for Spurs in the second round of the League Cup; but the North Londoners enjoyed a lot more success in the F.A. Cup. Altrincham, Wrexham and Oldham Athletic were all side-stepped before Manchester United proved too big an obstacle at the quarter-final stage. The Red Devils eventually triumphing 2-0 in a replay at Old Trafford.

1979-1980 SEASON

Tottenham Hotspur also reached the sixth round of the F.A. Cup in 1979-80. En route they beat Manchester United (in another Old Trafford replay) together with Swindon Town and Birmingham City. Liverpool halted the run with a single goal success at White Hart Lane. Manchester United had earlier tipped Spurs out of the League Cup, at the second round stage.

The first three 1979-80 League fixtures ended in defeat, with the defence leaking a total of ten goals. However, Keith Burkinshaw's side began to show better application, losing just once more during the next 12 fixtures. A run of five wins from six games propelled Spurs into fifth spot in mid-November. Sadly, they could not build on their good autumn form and faded back into mid-division, finishing in 14th place.

Three men – Barry Daines, Milija Aleksic and Mark Kendall – shared the goalkeeper's jersey, but none had the stamp of quality. One man who certainly did was Glenn Hoddle, who was the top scorer (with 19 goals) from midfield. Chris Jones netted nine goals, but no other player contributed a tally greater than four. John Pratt (332 League appearances – 39 goals) and Terry Naylor (243) played for the club for the last time in 1979-80.

1980-81 SEASON

With Glenn Hoddle increasing in stature and the arrival of two hungry strikers – Steve Archibald from Aberdeen and Stoke's Garth Crooks – Tottenham Hotspur were a much more effective force in 1980-81. Hoddle scored 12 times and Crooks 16, but the leading scorer was Archibald (with 20), who was the Division's joint top scorer. Spurs coasted through 1980-81 in mid-table and eventually finished in tenth place.

The 1980-81 campaign lingers long in the memories of many Spurs fans. This was because of two long cup runs – one that reached a disappointing conclusion and one that saw the collection of the club's 12th major trophy.

Three London sides – Orient, Crystal Palace and Arsenal – were defeated en route to the quarter-final stage of the League Cup. However, a fourth London club, West Ham United, halted this run with a 1-0 victory at White Hart Lane.

The League Cup run turned out to be merely a prelude, though, to an exciting tilt at the F.A. Cup. And it culminated in them ending their 14 year wait to lift the trophy. Coventry City and three lower Division sides were side-stepped to set up a semi-final meeting with Wolverhampton Wanderers. After a 2-2 draw at Hillsborough, Spurs got the upper hand in a Highbury replay, with Crooks netting a brace and Ricky Villa thumping the third in a 3-0 success.

The other finalists were John Bond's Manchester City and it was the Citizens who opened the scoring at Wembley Stadium through Tommy Hutchison shortly before the half-hour mark. The Scot was later accredited with the equaliser when he deflected a 79th minute free-kick from Hoddle into his own net. Neither side could break the deadlock in extra-time to set up a replay. That second game between the teams was played the following Thursday and was the first F.A. Cup final replay to be staged at Wembley.

Burkinshaw's tenacious side just edged that second see-saw encounter. Ricky Villa lashed the ball home to open the scoring early on, but City levelled and early in the second half City took a 2-1 lead. Spurs responded with some fine football and Crooks finished off an excellent piece of work by Hoddle to equalise with 20 minutes remaining. Then, six minutes later, Ricky Villa struck a majestic winner to decide the 100th F.A. Cup Final. The Argentinian collected a pass from Tony Galvin 35 yards from goal and set off on a dazzling run that mesmerised City's defence, before placing the ball between keeper Joe Corrigan's legs, to ignite a boom of joy from the Tottenham contingent. A sixth F.A. Cup was in the bag and a seventh was to be only twelve months away.

1981-1982 SEASON

The 1981-82 F.A. Cup winning side contained eight members of the previous season's successful team: skipper Steve Perryman, Chris Hughton, Paul Miller, Graham Roberts, Glenn Hoddle, Tony Galvin, Steve Archibald and Garth Crooks. Milija Aleksic had been replaced by former Anfield custodian Ray Clemence, while the two Argentinians (though contributing in the earlier rounds) missed the 1982 Final because of the Falklands War. Paul Price and Micky Hazard stepped into the breach, while a second winners' medal went to perennial substitute Garry Brooke.

The road to Wembley was paved with five tough matches in 1982. Arsenal, Leeds

United and Aston Villa were all defeated 1-0 at White Hart Lane, while Chelsea were edged out 3-2 in an even fiercer encounter at Stamford Bridge. A goal by Crooks and an own-goal ended Leicester City's hopes in the semi-final at Villa Park to set up an all London Final with Second Division QPR, managed by former Spurs midfielder (and future boss) Terry Venables.

Although firm favourites, Terry Burkinshaw's side failed to break the deadlock until Hoddle netted ten minutes before the end of extra-time. Yet, there was still time for Terry Fenwick (who was later to move to White Hart Lane) to head Rangers level. An early penalty from the cool Hoddle decided the replay, although the match failed to stir the pulses. Nevertheless, it was welcome reward for considerable hard graft in 1981-82, a campaign that had one time promised to be even more profitable as Spurs made a determined bid for silverware on four fronts.

Tottenham's first visit to Wembley Stadium in 1982 was for the League Cup Final against Liverpool. The Londoners previously disposed of Manchester United, Wrexham, Nottingham Forest and West Bromwich Albion (with just one goal deciding the two tight semi-final ties).

Archibald opened the scoring during the first half of the final, but Liverpool fought back and eventually took the trophy 3-1 after extra-time.

The European Cup Winners' Cup run was halted by Barcelona at the semi-final stage. Ajax (6-1 on aggregate), Dundalk and Eintracht Frankfurt were side-stepped en route, but after drawing 1-1 in London, the Catalonian side progressed after a single goal victory at the Nou Camp.

Spurs had their best League campaign for 11 seasons in 1981-82 when they finished fourth. They went more than four months without being beaten (from mid-December), but three successive defeats at the tail-end prevented them from taking third spot. 13-goal Crooks was the top scorer, while the stylish Hoddle contributed another ten goals.

To underline just what a fantastic campaign 1981-82 was for the club, skipper Steve Perryman was named as the 'Footballer of the Year'.

During 1981-82, in the game with Manchester City, Ally Dick made his debut at the age of 16 years and 301 days – to become the youngest man to represent Spurs in the Football League.

1982-1983 SEASON

Spurs also finished in fourth place in 1982-83. A mid-table finish looked more likely, though, but nine of the final 12 fixtures ended in victory to earn UEFA Cup qualification. Steve Archibald was the leading scorer (with 11 goals), while Gary

Mabbutt contributed a tally of ten from midfield.

To the great disappointment of their fans, Tottenham completely missed out on silverware in 1982-83. Second Division Burnley surprisingly ended their League Cup run (by a 4-1 scoreline) in a quarter-final replay at White Hart Lane. While, after dismissing Coleraine, Spurs were comprehensively ejected from the European Cup Winners' Cup by Bayern Munich in the second round. And, even more painfully, Tottenham Hotspur's first F.A. Cup defeat for nearly three years came in the fifth round at Everton.

1983-1984 SEASON

Tottenham dropped four places to eighth place in 1983-84. An unbeaten run of nine games (containing seven victories) lifted them to fourth place by the end of November. However, they could not sustain that fine form and ended the League campaign on a somewhat disappointing note with just four points from five fixtures. 21-goal Steve Archibald was the club's main marksman, while Mark Falco found the net 13 times.

Spurs fell at the second hurdle in each of the domestic cup competitions. Arsenal defeated them 2-1 at White Hart Lane and Norwich City proved too good for them in an F.A. Cup fourth round replay.

Disenchanted with the situation in the boardroom, Keith Burkinshaw announced during 1983-84 that he would resign at the end of that season. To wave him farewell, his side lifted another trophy – the UEFA Cup – the third piece of silverware collected while the Yorkshireman was at the helm.

After defeating Drogheda, they took on old rivals Feyenoord in the second round. Tottenham won the first leg 4-2 and then triumphed 2-0 in Rotterdam. Despite losing the away leg 1-0, they also performed marvellously in the third round against Bayern Munich and progressed with two goals at White Hart Lane. Further victories over Austria Vienna and Hajduk Split (on away goals) set up a two-legged Final with Anderlecht.

Both matches ended 1-1 with Paul Miller scoring in Belgium and Graham Roberts getting his name on the score-sheet in the return at White Hart Lane. The tie was still dead-locked at the end of extra-time and the destination of the trophy had to be decided by penalties. Keith Burkinshaw's boys showed the cooler nerves and triumphed 4-3 in the shoot-out to ensure Tottenham Hotspur lifted the UEFA Cup for the second time.

KEITH BURKINSHAW

Reign: 1976-1984

Honours: UEFA Cup and F.A. Cup (twice)

Highest League finish: 4th in 1981-82 and 1982-83

Best F.A. Cup Run: Winners in 1980-81 and 1981-82

Best League Cup Run: Final in 1981-82

Best European Run: UEFA Cup Winners in 1983-84

1984-1985 SEASON

Keith Burkinshaw's assistant Peter Shreeves stepped up to be the manager and, in his first season at the helm, Spurs finished in an even higher position than his former boss had ever managed. Wonderfully consistent, they were never out of the top five and actually led the table over the Christmas period. Eventually Everton raced clear at the top and an untimely 5-1 home defeat against Watford, in match 40, effectively stopped Spurs being the runners-up. Liverpool nudged them into third place on goal difference. However, Tottenham's 1984-85 tally of 77 points was a club record.

The side was extremely settled with the following ten men featuring in over two-thirds of the fixtures: Ray Clemence, Gary Stevens, Chris Hughton, Graham Roberts, Paul Miller, Steve Perryman, John Chiedozie, Tony Galvin, Glenn Hoddle and the First Division's third highest scorer Mark Falco (who bagged 22 goals). Garth Crooks scored in six consecutive League games and ended the season as the club's second top scorer on the 10-goal mark.

The fourth round proved to be Tottenham Hotspur's undoing in all three cups in 1985-86. Sunderland ended their League Cup hopes, while Liverpool knocked them out of the F.A. Cup at Anfield. And, not for the first time, their European aspirations were ended by a Spanish side. After defeating Sporting Braga, FC Bruges and Bohemians Prague, an own goal by Perryman proved fatal against Real Madrid in the quarter-final first leg at White Hart Lane. It proved to be the only strike in the 180 minutes and, sadly, the UEFA Cup slipped out of the possession of Tottenham Hotspur.

1985-1986 SEASON

There was to be no cup joy in 1985-86 either. Portsmouth knocked them out of the League Cup in a fourth round second replay. While Everton proved too good for them in the fifth round of the F.A. Cup at White Hart Lane.

Mark Falco netted 19 times to be the club's leading League goalscorer again in 1985-86. While, in his first season at the club, Chris Waddle netted 11 times. Tottenham hovered in mid-table for the bulk of the season and it took nine victories during the final 13 games to secure as high a position as tenth. It was not enough, however, to save the jobs of Shreeves or his assistant John Pratt. Another man who left the club in 1985-86 was Steve Perryman, who transferred to Oxford, after making a club record 655 League appearances (31 goals).

PETER SHREEVES

Reign: 1984-1986 and 1991-92
Honours: None
Highest League finish: 3rd in 1984-85
Best F.A. Cup Run: Round 5 in 1985-86
Best League Cup Run: Round 4 in 1984-85 and 1985-86
Best European Run: UEFA Cup Quarter-final in 1984-85
Best European Run: European Cup Winners' Cup Quarter-final in 1991-92

1986-1987 SEASON

The new man in the manager's office at the start of the 1986-87 campaign was David Pleat, who was reluctantly released by Luton Town. His plan to use Clive Allen as the spearhead of the attack paid immediate dividends. The striker scored an amazing 49 goals in all competitions including 33 in the Football League. It was not surprising that Allen was the country's leading scorer and he was also named as the 'Footballer of the Year'. However, despite giving all three competitions a good tilt, Spurs' failure to land a trophy frustrated their fans.

Pleat's side gave a good account of themselves in the First Division, with nine wins from eleven matches lifting them into the top four in early March. They could not quite keep up the momentum, though, and collected just seven points from as many fixtures at the tail-end of the campaign to finish third, six points behind second placed Liverpool and 15 points behind the champions Everton. Graham Roberts (209 League appearances – 23 goals) left White Hart Lane for Rangers during the 1986-87 season. While Tony Galvin (201 – 20) and Paul Miller (208 – 7) also made their last League appearances for the club.

Spurs reached the last four of the League Cup after thrashing West Ham United 5-0 in a replay and appeared on course for another Wembley date for much of the two legged semi-final against Arsenal. Clive Allen netted the only goal at Highbury and also put his side into a two goal aggregate lead at White Hart Lane. However, the Gunners rallied to score twice and force extra-time. There were no further goals in that game, but Allen scored again in the replay at White Hart Lane to bring his total in the tournament to 12 – a record haul in one season. Sadly, for the Spurs faithful, their North London rivals netted twice and another trip to the 'Twin Towers' went begging.

Those fans did not have long to wait to visit Wembley, though, because their side went one better in the F.A. Cup. Scunthorpe United, Crystal Palace, Newcastle United and Wimbledon were all beaten to set up yet another Highbury semi-final. This time the opposition proved to be slightly less formidable and Watford were defeated 4-1.

Tottenham were fully expected to extend their record of never losing an F.A. Cup Final, but Coventry City failed to read the script and the course of history was altered in a five-goal thriller.

It begun promisingly enough when Clive Allen headed in after just two minutes. And, even though the Sky Blues equalised, Tottenham still went in at half-time in front courtesy of a goal by Gary Mabbutt. With Glenn Hoddle, in his last game in a Spurs shirt, surprisingly marked out of the game, Coventry took over to force extra-time and then snatched the cup when a cross-shot deflected past Ray Clemence off the unfortunate Mabbutt.

1987-1988 SEASON

After 377 League appearances (88 goals), Glenn Hoddle moved to Monaco in the summer of 1987. It was not long before two more significant departures severely impeded the club's progress. Spurs were lying in third place in early October when homesick skipper Richard Gough left suddenly for Glasgow Rangers. Then, later that same month, Pleat resigned following allegations about his private life. In addition, Chris Waddle missed a significant spell after being injured playing for England and Tottenham started to slide.

After a nine match winless run in which Spurs netted only three times, Terry Venables took over as manager. An improvement followed, but another poor patch near the end of the season ensured that their final position was only 13th. Clive Allen was the top goalscorer again in 1987-88, but his quota had been cut by exactly two-thirds to 11. Belgian striker Nico Claesen contributed 10 goals, but no other Spurs player registered more than four goals during the campaign. Ray Clemence made his 240th and last League appearance for Spurs in 1987-88.

Spurs' League Cup hopes were destroyed by Aston Villa, while Third Division Port Vale tipped them out of the F.A. Cup.

Ossie Ardiles was dogged by injuries during his later years in a Spurs shirt and he finally moved to QPR during May 1988 after making a total of 238 League appearances (16 goals). Then, in the summer of 1988, after netting a 60 goals in 105 games, Clive

Allen left for Bordeaux. But as one door banged shut, another was flung open when Paul Gascoigne arrived (from Newcastle United) for a record £2 million fee.

DAVID PLEAT

Reign: 1986-1987 and 2003-2004

Highest League finish: 3rd in 1986-87

Best F.A. Cup Run: Final in 1986-87

Best League Cup Run: Semi-final in 1986-87

1988-1989 SEASON

Terry Venables' side gradually improved after a poor start to 1988-89. They won only one of their first ten fixtures but, in contrast, won five of their last seven games to finish in sixth place. Chris Waddle top scored with 14 goals, two more than former Blackpool striker Paul Stewart.

Notts County and Blackburn Rovers were defeated in the League Cup, but this promising run came to an end at the Dell, where Southampton triumphed 2-1. A run in the F.A. Cup never materialised, with Second Division Bradford City winning 1-0 at Valley Parade.

1989-1990 SEASON

Although Chris Waddle had moved to Marseille during the summer, the fans looked forward to 1989-90 with great anticipation. Not least because Venables returned to his former club Barcelona to buy Gary Lineker. The England striker did not disappoint either, he enjoyed immediate success in North London and finished the season as the First Division's leading scorer (with 24 goals).

After another mediocre start to the campaign, Spurs gradually became much more consistent and eight victories in the last ten games lifted them into third place (with 63 points), behind champions Liverpool (79 points) and Aston Villa (70 points). Chris Hughton made his 297th and last League appearance (12 goals) in 1989-90.

Hopes of another Wembley appearance were raised when Tottenham reached the quarter-final of the League Cup, but Nottingham Forest edged them out by the odd goal in five in a White Hart Lane replay. Spurs fell at the first hurdle in the F.A. Cup, losing 3-1 at home to Southampton.

1990-1991 SEASON

Tottenham Hotspur made an unusually bright start to the campaign. They registered ten matches unbeaten and it was not until just before Christmas that they slipped out of the top three. However, they only won two of their last 20 League fixtures and had to be content with tenth place. Gary Lineker was again the top goalscorer (with 15); but he lacked support up front.

Terry Venables' side again reached the quarter-final of the League Cup; but disappointingly lost a replay against Chelsea by 3-0 at White Hart Lane. However, the 1990-91 campaign was ultimately a very successful one as the club lifted the F.A. Cup for a record eighth time.

Blackpool, Oxford United, Portsmouth and Notts County were despatched with style to take Spurs into the semi-final, where they were drawn to play Arsenal. For this big clash between the two great North London clubs, the F.A. opted to utilise Wembley. It was the first time that the stadium was used to stage a semi-final. Paul Gascoigne netted a marvellous free-kick as his side triumphed 3-1 to inflict one of three defeats on the Gunners (who later collected the title) in all competitions in 1990-91.

Gascoigne – in his last game before joining Lazio for a £5.5 million fee – made his mark less than 15 minutes into the Final, but unfortunately it was a negative one for Tottenham. The midfielder badly injured himself fouling Gary Charles and Forest took the lead through Stuart Pearce from the resultant free-kick. Nevertheless, it all came good eventually as Paul Stewart equalised early in the second half and, in extra-time, an own goal by Des Walker enabled Gary Mabbutt to raise the F.A. Cup aloft and so exorcise the demons of four years earlier.

The men who brought the F.A. Cup back to Tottenham in 1990-91 were the popular Norwegian goalkeeper Erik Thorstvedt, Justin Edinburgh, Pat Van Den Hauwe, Steve Sedgley, David Howells, Vinny Samways, Paul Allen, Mabbutt, Stewart, Gascoigne, Lineker (who had a second half penalty saved), Paul Walsh and Nayim. The two players named last came off the bench.

Despite winning the F.A. Cup, Spurs had severe financial problems and almost folded. The rescue package came from Terry Venables, who took a chief-executive role, and multi-millionaire businessman Alan Sugar who became the club's chairman.

TERRY VENABLES

Reign: 1987-1991
Honours: F.A. Cup
Highest League finish: 3rd in 1989-90
Best F.A. Cup Run: Winners in 1990-91
Best League Cup Run: Quarter-final in 1989-90 and 1990-91

1991-1992 SEASON

Terry Venables' move 'upstairs' paved the way for Peter Shreeves to rejoin as manager in July 1991. The team responded well initially, but failed to build on an encouraging start. A ten match winless run sent them spinning into relegation trouble. However, with the pressure building, they rallied to win five of their last ten games and earn safety in 15th place. The 'Footballer of the Year' Gary Lineker netted 28 times to become the First Division's second top scorer. The club's next highest goalscorer was Scottish striker Gordon Durie (with seven), in his first season after transferring from Chelsea.

Having lost their grip on the F.A. Cup (when beaten 2-1 at home by Aston Villa, in a third round replay) hopes of another trip to Wembley rested on their run in the League Cup. Spurs battled through to the semi-final and looked favourites to go further after drawing at the City Ground in the first leg. However, it was Nottingham Forest who shaded the second leg in London.

Tottenham supporters also enjoyed eight games in the European Cup Winners' Cup in 1991-92. Sadly, old rivals Feyenoord got the better of them in the quarter-final. A solitary goal in Rotterdam proving the difference over the 180 minutes. Stockerau, Hajduk Split and Porto had previously been defeated as Spurs built up a head of steam.

1992-1993 SEASON

Peter Shreeves left the club during the summer of 1992. Team affairs were handed over to coaches Doug Livermore and Ray Clemence, while Terry Venables became more active again in team selection. Whoever was picking the team the task was made a lot more difficult by not having Gary Lineker to call upon. He had signed for Japan's Grampus Eight during the summer of 1992. The former England captain had topped the club's list of scorers in each of his three seasons with the club – netting 67 times in his 105 League appearances.

Spurs made a poor start to 1992-93 and did not win until their sixth League game, but five successive victories in the new year helped them to finish eighth. Lineker's replacement was early season signing Teddy Sheringham, who finished as the Premier League's leading scorer with 22 goals (all but the first were netted while he wore a Tottenham shirt).

Sheringham's old club, Nottingham Forest, ended Tottenham's League Cup hopes at the fourth round stage. However, Spurs embarked on another good F.A. Cup run, defeating Marlow, Norwich City, Wimbledon and Manchester City to set up another Wembley semi-final meeting with Arsenal. This time it was the Gunners who booked a return trip to the Twin Towers, scoring the only goal in the second half.

The breakdown of the Venables/Sugar alliance saw the former leave the club at the end of the season along with Clemence. Ossie Ardiles returned to become manager, with another Tottenham legend Steve Perryman relinquishing the manager's office at Watford to become his assistant.

1993-1994 SEASON

Ossie Ardiles' new side made a good start to 1993-94 and were as high as fifth in mid-October. However, Spurs began to struggle and suffered a dire patch in which they won only twice in 23 matches, a spell which included seven successive defeats at the start of 1994 (a club record). Teddy Sheringham bagged 14 goals to be the leading scorer again, but his side had to be content with 15th place in the final table. Among the men to leave White Lane during 1993-94 was midfielder Paul Allen (292 League appearances – 23 goals), who joined Southampton.

Spurs enjoyed some success in the League Cup, but their run was eventually ended by Aston Villa at the quarter-final stage. While dreams of another lengthy F.A. Cup run evaporated at Portman Road in the fourth round.

1994-1995 SEASON

White Hart Lane was buzzing at the start of 1994-95 with the arrival of German striker Jürgen Klinsmann and Romanian Ilie Dumitrescu. The latter's compatriot Gica Popescu joined soon afterwards, by which time the fans had already experienced the roller-coaster of emotions with three wins (including a 4-3 opener at Sheffield Wednesday) and three defeats. Ardiles' attacking policy attracted a lot of comment from the press and on 1st November the board relieved him of his duties. The Argentinian's side had conceded 24 goals in 12 League games and a further nine in three League Cup ties – the last of which ended in a 3-0 exit at Notts County.

Caretaker boss Perryman reigned for one match, which ended in defeat, and he departed when Gerry Francis swapped the manager's office at Loftus Road for the one down Tottenham High Road. His first game was a 4-3 reverse at home by Aston Villa, but Francis soon tightened the defence and his side lost only five more League games during the final two-thirds of the campaign. It was remarkable how quickly the side were transformed and yet the new manager made no new signings.

Klinsmann, with his distinctive diving celebrations, quickly became the fans' favourite, while Teddy Sheringham, Darren Anderton, Nicky Barmby and David Howells played an important part in helping to keep the goals flowing. Spurs eventually finished seventh, with Klinsmann top scoring (with 20 goals) and

Sheringham netting 18 times.

The club's best performance of the campaign was a marvellous 2-1 victory at Anfield in the quarter-final of the F.A. Cup. Klinsmann netted the winner and also scored (from the spot) in the semi-final at Elland Road. However, much to the great disappointment of thousands of fans who travelled from London, that Sunday turned out to be the most unhappy day of the season as Everton ran out 4-1 winners.

Klinsmann was named as the 'Footballer of the Year'. However, to the disappointment of millions of English football fans, soon afterwards he returned to his homeland to join Bayern Munich.

OSSIE ARDILES

Reign: 1993-1994
Honours: None
Highest League finish: 15th in 1993-94
Best F.A. Cup Run: Round 4 in 1993-94
Best League Cup Run: Quarter-final in 1993-94

1995-1996 SEASON

Tottenham Hotspur slipped one place to eighth in 1995-96, with the ever-present Teddy Sheringham the top scorer with 16 goals. His new strike partner, Chris Armstrong (signed from Crystal Palace), contributed 15. After a shaky start, Spurs rose from mid-table to sit among the top four during December and January. They drifted afterwards; but only lost nine League games all term and conceded more than one goal on just nine occasions.

Coventry City defeated Spurs in the League Cup, while Nottingham Forest knocked them out of the F.A. Cup, following a penalty shoot-out at the end of a fifth round replay at White Hart Lane. Spurs also played four Intertoto Cup ties at the start of 1995-96. They lost three of these games (against FC Koln, FC Luzern and Tster), but won at Rudar. The two 'home' games were played at Brighton's Goldstone Ground and the very inexperienced Tottenham squad finished fourth in their group.

1996-1997 SEASON

A catalogue of injuries torpedoed hopes of lifting any silverware in 1996-97. Skipper Gary Mabbutt broke his leg in the first game, while Darren Anderton and Chris Armstrong missed large chunks of the season. Even new signings like Norwegian striker Steffen Iversen, John Scales and Ramon Vega were side-lined at various stages. Spurs finished in 10th place. Teddy Sheringham was yet again the leading goalscorer, but he found the net just seven times, with the side as a whole only managing 44 League goals.

Manchester United proved too tough in the F.A. Cup and the only cup victories came in the League Cup. That run came to a juddering halt in the fourth round when Bolton Wanderers thrashed them 6-1 at Burnden Park.

1997-1998 SEASON

To the despair of the bulk of the fans, Teddy Sheringham moved on during the summer of 1997. The England striker joined Manchester United for £3.5 million. Partially placating the supporters, Gerry Francis made two big signings from Newcastle United. David Ginola was signed for a £2.5 million fee, while England striker Les Ferdinand cost £6 million.

Ferdinand netted three times in August, but in total they only found the net six times in the first ten League matches. Spurs dropped to 16th place after a 4-0 defeat at Anfield in early November and Francis resigned later that same month. His replacement was Christian Gross, coach of the Zurich based Grasshoppers.

Two men returned to White Hart Lane in December – David Pleat (following his sacking at Sheffield Wednesday) and Jürgen Klinnsman. The former took the position as Director of Football, while the German helped galvanise things on the pitch.

Spurs were second from bottom in mid-January and did not pull away from relegation trouble until the season's end. Klinsmann was the top scorer, with nine – four of which came in the penultimate game, at Wimbledon, which was won 6-2. Tottenham eventually finished in 14th place, but only accumulated four points more than relegated Bolton Wanderers.

Fellow Premiership sides, Derby County and Barnsley, ended Spurs' cup hopes, in the League Cup and F.A. Cup, respectively.

Klinsmann left North London again at the end of the season. Among the others who pulled on a Spurs shirt for the last time in 1997-98 were club captain Gary Mabbutt (477 League appearances – 27 goals) and popular midfielder David Howells (277 – 22).

GERRY FRANCIS

Reign: 1994-1997
Highest League finish: 7th in 1994-95
Best F.A. Cup Run: Semi-final in 1994-95
Best League Cup Run: Round 4 in 1996-97 and 1997-98
Best European Run: Intertoto Cup First Group Stage in 1995-96

1998-1999 SEASON

Tottenham Hotspur made an indifferent start to 1998-99 and Christian Gross offered his resignation, after an unhappy ten months at the helm. On 1st October Leeds boss George Graham (whose managerial fame was achieved with Arsenal) signed a four-year contract to be the manager of Spurs.

Graham's side made little impact in the League. Their highest position was eighth at the end of October and they eventually finished 11th. At one point they strung together six consecutive draws – four of which were goalless – a club record sequence. Steffen Iversen was the top scorer, with nine goals.

After seven barren seasons, Graham managed to bring silverware to White Hart Lane at the first attempt when his side lifted the League Cup. Brentford, Northampton Town, Liverpool, Manchester United and Wimbledon were all beaten en route to a Wembley final with Leicester City.

Spurs were handicapped by the sending-off of Justin Edinburgh and the very tight and tense encounter looked set for extra-time when Allan Nielsen popped up to head in the only goal in injury-time. The victorious players at Wembley on 21st March were goalkeeper Ian Walker, Stephen Carr, Steffen Freund, Ramon Vega, Sol Campbell, Darren Anderton, Les Ferdinand, David Ginola, Edinburgh, Iversen, Nielsen and substitute Andy Sinton. The Worthington Cup became the 16th major trophy won by Tottenham Hotspur and guaranteed their fans another season of European football.

The North Londoners nearly collected a second piece of silverware in 1988-99 as they got as far as the semi-final stage of the F.A. Cup. A splendid goal by Ginola (who was later named as the 'Footballer of the Year') was enough to kill off Barnsley in the quarter-final, but Spurs then lost 2-0 to Newcastle United at Old Trafford.

CHRISTIAN GROSS

Reign: 1997-1998
Honours: None
Highest League finish: 14th in 1997-98
Best F.A. Cup Run: Round 4 in 1997-98
Best League Cup Run: None

1999-2000 SEASON

Spurs' UEFA Cup run turned out to be a disappointingly short affair. After Zimbru Chisinau were beaten in the first round, a Steffen Iversen penalty proved to be the only goal of the second round first leg against Kaierslautern. However, two very late goals (the second an own-goal by Stephen Carr) gave the Germans a 2-1 aggregate success.

There was little joy in the two domestic cups either. Tottenham's hold on the League Cup slipped when they crashed 3-1 at Fulham in the fourth round. While Newcastle United thrashed them 6-1 in an F.A. Cup third round replay.

Tottenham spent most of 1999-2000 in the top half of the Premiership table. They were in sixth spot after beating Liverpool at White Hart Lane in early January. But they gradually slipped down the table and only finished as high as tenth by winning three of their last five fixtures. Iversen and Chris Armstrong were the club's joint leading scorers, on the 14-goal mark. Among the men who left the club in 1999-2000 was Justin Edinburgh (213 League appearances – 1 goal), who joined Portsmouth.

2000-2001 SEASON

Spurs were among the Premiership leaders during the early part of the 2000-01 campaign. However, they gradually dropped back into mid-division. A 4-2 victory over Newcastle at the turn of the year suggested better things, but George Graham's side immediately registered four successive goalless draws.

With Alan Sugar selling his interest in the club, the was a new dawn at White Hart Lane with ENIC buying the club. An early casualty of the new regime was George Graham, who was dismissed after a meeting with new executive vice-chairman David Buchler.

Glenn Hoddle, the former England manager and Tottenham legend, was appointed as the new manager. Hoddle, and his assistant John Gorman (another former Spurs player), resigned from similar posts at Southampton to return to White Hart Lane. One of the new manager's first tasks was to oversee the F.A. Cup semi-final with Arsenal at Old Trafford. Although Gary Doherty opened the scoring, the Gunners scored a goal in each half to progress to the Final in Cardiff. Earlier in 2000-01, Spurs exited the League Cup at home to Birmingham City.

Tottenham finished the 2000-01 on a high note by beating Manchester United 3-1 at home and finished 12th in the table. Les Ferdinand was the club's top scorer (with 10 goals). In his first term in London, Sergei Rebrov contributed nine goals, but no other Spurs player netted more than three times during the course of the season.

Sol Campbell moved across North London during the summer of 2001, when he signed for Arsenal. The stylish central defender had netted ten times in 255 League appearances for Spurs. Another man to leave White Hart Lane during the summer of

2001 was goalkeeper Ian Walker, who joined Leicester City (after making 259 League appearances).

GEORGE GRAHAM

Reign: 1998-2001
Honours: League Cup
Highest League finish: 10th in 1999-2000
Best F.A. Cup Run: Semi-final in 1998-99 and 2000-01
Best League Cup Run: Winners in 1998-99
Best European Run: UEFA Cup Round 2 in 1999-2000

2001-2002 SEASON

Glenn Hoddle's side made a sluggish start to 2001-02, winning only two of their first eight League fixtures. However, they climbed to seventh spot by the end of November and continued to bob along in the lower reaches of the top half of the table for the remainder of the campaign. They eventually finished ninth. Gus Poyet and the returning Teddy Sheringham were the joint top scorers, with 10 goals apiece. West Ham-bound Les Ferdinand netted nine times in his last campaign at the Lane to bring his tally to 33 goals from 118 League appearances.

For a few weeks of 2001-02 the Spurs faithful had high hopes of their side lifting two trophies. Hoddle's side side-stepped Torquay United, Tranmere Rovers, Fulham, Bolton Wanderers and Chelsea en route to a League Cup Final meeting with Blackburn Rovers. Spurs arrived at Cardiff's Millennium Stadium as slight favourites; but were not quite strong enough on the day.

Matt Jansen put Rovers ahead midway through the first half; but Christian Ziege netted an equaliser eight minutes later. Sadly, the only goal of the second period was netted by Blackburn's Andy Cole and the Worthington Cup slipped away from Tottenham's hands. All hopes of a quick return to Cardiff evaporated, the following month, when Chelsea ran out 4-0 winners at White Hart Lane in an F.A. Cup fifth round replay.

2002-2003 SEASON

Tottenham Hotspur stood proudly at the top of the Premiership after four games of 2002-03. Hoddle's side gradually slipped down the table, but were always in the top half. The season ended on a low with three successive defeats, including a 5-1 thrashing at Middlesbrough and a 4-0 reverse at home to Blackburn Rovers. They finished tenth with Robbie Keane, an early season buy from Leeds United, top scoring with 13 goals. Teddy Sheringham netted another 12 times to close his Tottenham career with 97 League goals from 236 appearances (in two spells), before signing for Portsmouth.

Spurs crashed out of both cups at the third round stage. They lost 2-1 at First Division Burnley in the League Cup and were dumped out of the F.A. Cup 4-0 in a Saturday evening clash by Hoddle's old club Southampton.

2003-2004 SEASON

During the summer of 2003, Glenn Hoddle recruited Stephane Dalmat, Mbulelo Mabizela, Bobby Zamora and Frederic Kanoute. However, with his side winning just one of their first six League fixtures, Hoddle soon lost his job. The board appointed David Pleat as caretaker manager (assisted by coach Chris Hughton). It was a role that Pleat held on to for the remainder of the campaign.

Spurs were rather undistinguished for much of 2003-04. Their best spell came just after Christmas when they won five out of six League fixtures. Nevertheless, they fell away badly and in fact, their form became so poor, they were in serious danger of being relegated.

However, that stock of points gained in January were to prove to be invaluable and Pleat's side ended the campaign on a high note with two successive victories (against Blackburn Rovers and Wolves). Tottenham's position in the final table was 14th, 12 points clear of the three relegated clubs. 14-goal Robbie Keane was the club's leading scorer, while the ex-West Ham United pair of Kanoute and Jermain Defoe netted seven goals apiece. Defoe and midfielder Michael Brown moved to White Hart Lane during the January transfer window. Zamora joined the Hammers as a makeweight in the deal after failing to score in the League for Spurs.

Tottenham reached the last eight of the League Cup by beating Coventry City, West Ham and Manchester City. They came within four minutes of reaching the last four when Middlesbrough equalised at White Hart Lane. The quarter-final was eventually decided by a penalty shoot-out, which Middlesbrough (the eventual winners of the competition) won 5-4. Pleat's side crashed out of the F.A. Cup at the end of a thrilling fourth round replay with Manchester City at White Hart Lane. Spurs looked comfortable winners when they led 3-0 at half-time, but much to the astonishment of their fans they allowed City to net four times to claim victory.

There were to be great changes at White Hart Lane during the summer of 2004. The squad was immediately boosted by the arrival of goalkeeper Paul Robinson (from Leeds United). More significantly, Frank Arnesen was appointed sporting director (with David Pleat leaving the club) and Jacques Santini (the coach of the French national squad) was installed as the new manager. Tottenham Hotspur fans looked forward to 2004-05 with genuine belief that their team would enjoy a much better campaign.

GLENN HODDLE

Reign: 2001-2003
Honours: None
Highest League finish: 9th in 2001-02
Best F.A. Cup Run: Semi-final in 2000-01 – Glenn Hoddle became manager after the quarter-final and oversaw the semi-final defeat.
Best League Cup Run: Final in 2001-02

1974-75

#	Month	Date	V	Opponent	Res	Score	Scorers	Attendance
1	Aug	17	(h)	Ipswich T	L	0-1		26,444
2		21	(a)	Manchester C	L	0-1		31,549
3		24	(a)	Carlisle U	L	0-1		18,426
4		28	(h)	Manchester C	L	1-2	Peters	20,079
5		31	(h)	Derby Co	W	2-0	Neighbour 2	20,676
6	Sep	7	(a)	Liverpool	L	2-5	Perryman, Chivers	47,538
7		14	(h)	West Ham U	W	2-1	England, Chivers	27,959
8		21	(a)	Wolverhampton W	W	3-2	Chivers 2, Peters	20,647
9		28	(h)	Middlesbrough	L	1-2	Neighbour	23,282
10	Oct	5	(h)	Burnley	L	2-3	Pratt, England	18,441
11		12	(a)	Chelsea	L	0-1		32,660
12		16	(h)	Carlisle U	D	1-1	Chivers	12,813
13		19	(h)	Arsenal	W	2-0	Perryman, Chivers	36,294
14		26	(a)	Luton T	D	1-1	Chivers	22,420
15	Nov	2	(a)	Stoke C	D	2-2	Duncan 2	24,667
16		9	(h)	Everton	D	1-1	Chivers	29,052
17		16	(a)	Leicester C	W	2-1	Coates, Peters	23,244
18		23	(h)	Birmingham C	D	0-0		27,761
19		30	(a)	Sheffield U	W	1-0	Duncan	20,289
20	Dec	4	(a)	Leeds U	L	1-2	Duncan	25,832
21		7	(h)	Newcastle U	W	3-0	Knowles 2, Chivers	23,422
22		14	(a)	Ipswich T	L	0-4		20,812
23		21	(h)	Queen's Park R	L	1-2	Duncan	21,150
24		26	(a)	West Ham U	D	1-1	Peters	37,682
25		28	(h)	Coventry C	D	1-1	Smith (og)	20,307
26	Jan	11	(a)	Newcastle U	W	5-2	Knowles, Conn 3, Duncan	39,679
27		18	(h)	Sheffield U	L	1-3	Duncan	15,812
28	Feb	1	(a)	Everton	L	0-1		40,912
29		8	(h)	Stoke C	L	0-2		22,941
30		15	(a)	Coventry C	D	1-1	Duncan	15,227
31		18	(a)	Birmingham C	L	0-1		24,240
32		22	(h)	Leicester C	L	0-3		20,937
33	Mar	1	(a)	Derby Co	L	1-3	Jones	22,995
34		15	(a)	Middlesbrough	L	0-3		25,637
35		22	(h)	Liverpool	L	0-2		34,331
36		28	(h)	Wolverhampton W	W	3-0	Perryman 2, Duncan	27,238
37		29	(a)	Queen's Park R	W	1-0	Duncan	25,461
38	Apr	5	(h)	Luton T	W	2-1	Conn, Duncan	25,796
39		12	(a)	Burnley	L	2-3	Perryman, Duncan	17,865
40		19	(h)	Chelsea	W	2-0	Conn, Perryman	50,998
41		26	(a)	Arsenal	L	0-1		43,762
42		28	(h)	Leeds U	W	4-2	Knowles 2 (1 pen), Conn, Chivers	49,886

FINAL LEAGUE POSITION: 19th in Division One

Appearances

Sub. Appearances

Goals

Jennings	Evans	Naylor	England	Osgood	Coates	McGrath	Perryman	Jones	Peters	Neighbour	Beal	Pratt	Chivers	Knowles	Duncan	McNab	Conn	Kinnear	Daines	McAllister	
1	2	3	4	5	6	7	8	9	10	11											1
1	2	3		5	4	7	8	9	10	11	6										2
1	2	3	5		6	12	8	9*	10	11	4	7									3
1	2	3	5		4	7	8		10	11	6		9								4
1	2	3	5		11		8		10	7	6	4	9								5
1	2	3	5*		11	12	8		10	7	6	4	9								6
1	2		5		11		8		10	7	6	4	9	3							7
1	2	12	5		11		8		10*	7	6	4	9	3							8
1	2		5		11		8		10	7	6	4	9	3							9
1	2		5		11	10	8			7	6	4	9	3							10
1	2	11	5				8	10		7	6	4	9	3							11
1	2	6	5		11		8	10		7		4	9	3							12
1	2	6	5		12		8*	11	10	7		4	9	3							13
1	2	6	5		12		8		10	7*		4	9	3	11						14
1	2	6	5		7		8		10		3	4	9		11						15
1	2	6	5		7		8		10	12	3*	4	9		11						16
1	2	6	5		7		8		10		3	4	9		11						17
1	2	6	5		7	12	8		10		3	4*	9		11						18
1	2	6	5		7		8		10			4	9	3	11						19
1	2	6	5		7		8		10			4	9	3	11						20
1		6	5		7		8		10		2		9*	3	11	4	12				21
1		6	5		7	9	8		10		2	12		3	11	4*					22
1		6	5		7		8		10	12	2*	4	9	3	11						23
1		6	5		7		8		10			4	9	3	11			2			24
1		6	5		7		8		10	12		4	9*	3	11			2			25
1	12	6	5				8		10	7*	4			3	11		9	2			26
1		6	5				8		10	7	4			3	11		9	2			27
1		6	5				8		10		4	3	9		11		7	2			28
		6	5		12		8		10*		4	2	9	3	11		7		1		29
1		6	5				8		10				9	3	11		7	2		4	30
1		6	5		12		8		10				9	3	11		7	2		4	31
1		6	5				8		10	12			9	3	11		7	2		4	32
1		6		10			8	9			5			3	11		7	2		4	33
1		6		10			8	9			5			3	11		7	2		4	34
1		6	5	10	12		8	9					3*		11		7	2		4	35
1		6	5				8	9		11	4			3	10		7	2			36
1		6	5				8	9		11	4	7		3	10		2*			12	37
1			5				8	9		11*	4	6	12	3	10		7	2			38
1		6	5	10			8	9			4			3	11		7	2			39
1		6	5				8	9		11	4			3	10		7	2			40
1		6	5				8	9		11*	4	12		3	10		7	2			41
1		6	5				8	10			4	11	9	3			7	2			42
41	20	37	31	10	26	5	42	16	29	21	28	27	27	31	28	2	16	17	1	7	
	1	1			4	4				4		2	1				1			1	
			2		1		6	1	4	3		1	10	5	12		6				

27

1975-76

1	Aug	16	(h)	Middlesbrough	W	1-0	Perryman	25,502
2		20	(h)	Ipswich T	D	1-1	Duncan	28,351
3		23	(a)	Liverpool	L	2-3	Jones, Duncan	42,729
4		25	(a)	West Ham U	L	0-1		36,567
5		30	(h)	Norwich C	D	2-2	Pratt, Duncan	23,140
6	Sep	6	(a)	Manchester U	L	2-3	Chivers, Jones	51,641
7		13	(h)	Derby Co	L	2-3	Chivers, Duncan	28,455
8		20	(a)	Leeds	D	1-1	Pratt	27,372
9		27	(h)	Arsenal	D	0-0		37,064
10	Oct	4	(a)	Newcastle U	D	2-2	Pratt, Duncan	33,290
11		11	(a)	Aston Villa	D	1-1	Pratt	40,048
12		18	(h)	Manchester C	D	2-2	Jones 2	30,554
13		25	(a)	Leicester C	W	3-2	Coates, Perryman, Chivers	22,088
14	Nov	1	(h)	Wolverhampton W	W	2-1	Young, Neighbour	26,102
15		8	(a)	Queen's Park R	D	0-0		28,434
16		15	(h)	Stoke C	D	1-1	Jones	25,698
17		22	(a)	Manchester C	L	1-2	Osgood	31,457
18		29	(h)	Burnley	W	2-1	Duncan 2	21,222
19	Dec	6	(a)	Sheffield U	W	2-1	Duncan 2	22,949
20		10	(h)	Everton	D	2-2	Pratt, Duncan	18,638
21		13	(h)	Liverpool	L	0-4		29,891
22		20	(a)	Middlesbrough	L	0-1		22,046
23		26	(h)	Birmingham C	L	1-3	Chivers (pen)	21,651
24		27	(a)	Coventry C	D	2-2	Duncan 2	21,125
25	Jan	10	(a)	Derby Co	W	3-2	McAllister, Perryman, Neighbour	28,085
26		17	(h)	Manchester U	D	1-1	Duncan	49,185
27		31	(a)	Ipswich T	W	2-1	Osgood (pen), Coates	24,049
28	Feb	7	(h)	West Ham U	D	1-1	Duncan	32,832
29		14	(h)	Queen's Park R	L	0-3		28,190
30		21	(a)	Stoke C	W	2-1	Hoddle, Duncan	17,110
31		24	(a)	Everton	L	0-1		18,126
32		28	(h)	Leicester C	D	1-1	Chivers	21,427
33	Mar	6	(a)	Norwich C	L	1-3	Chivers	20,460
34		13	(h)	Aston Villa	W	5-2	McAllister, Perryman, Duncan, Robinson, Nicholl (og)	24,169
35		16	(a)	Wolverhampton W	W	1-0	Pratt	21,544
36		20	(a)	Burnley	W	2-1	Pratt, Duncan	15,490
37		27	(h)	Sheffield U	W	5-0	Young, Perryman 2, Chivers, Duncan	21,370
38	Apr	3	(a)	Arsenal	W	2-0	Pratt, Duncan	42,031
39		10	(h)	Leeds U	D	0-0		40,365
40		17	(a)	Birmingham C	L	1-3	Pratt	30,616
41		19	(h)	Coventry C	W	4-1	Pratt, Osgood, Duncan, Neighbour	21,107
42		24	(h)	Newcastle U	L	0-3		29,649

FINAL LEAGUE POSITION: 9th in Division One

Appearances

Sub. Appearances

Goals

Jennings	Kinnear	Naylor	Pratt	Osgood	McAlister	McNab	Perryman	Chivers	Jones	Neighbour	Knowles	Duncan	Conn	Smith	Hoddle	Young	Coates	McGrath	Walford	Stead	Robinson	Brotherston	Daines	#
1	2	3	4	5	6	7	8	9	10	11														1
1		2*	4	5	6	7	8	9	10	11	3	12												2
1		2	4	5	6		8	9	10		3	11	7											3
1		2	4	5	6	12	8	9	10		3	11*	7											4
1		8	4	5	6	7		10	9		3*	11	12	2										5
1		3	4	5	6	7	8	12	10	11		9		2*										6
1		3	2	5	6	7	8	4	10	11		9												7
1		2	4	6		7	8		10	11	3	9				5								8
1		2	4	6		7	8	12	10	11	3	9*				5								9
1		2	4	6		7	8		10	11	3*	9				5	12							10
1		2	4	6	3		8	12	10	11		9*	7			5								11
1			4	6	2		8	9		11		10	7			5	3							12
1			4	6	2		8	9		11		10	7			5	3							13
1		2	12	6	3		8	9		11		10	7*			5	4							14
1		2	4	6	3		8	9*	12	11		10				5	7							15
1		2	4	6	3*		8	9		11		10				5	7	12						16
1		2	4	6	3		8	9*	12	11		10				5	7							17
1		2	4	6	3	12	8	9		11*		10				5	7							18
1		2	4	6	3		8	9		11		10				5	7							19
1		2	4	6	3	12	8	9		11		10				5	7*							20
1		2	4	6	3	7	8	9		11		10*				5	12							21
1		2	4	6	3		8	9		11		10				5	7							22
1		2	4	6	3	11	8	9	12			10				5	7*							23
1		2	4	6	3		8	9	12	11		10				5	7*							24
1		2	4	6	3		8	9		11		10				5	7							25
1		2	4	6	3		8	9		11		10				5	7							26
1			4	6	3		8	9		11		10				5	7		2					27
1		2	4	6	3		8	9	12	11*		10				5	7							28
1		2	4	6	3		8	9	12	11		10				5	7*							29
1			4	6	3		8	9*	12	11		10			7	5			2					30
1			4	6	3		8	9		11		10			7	5			2					31
1		2	4*	6			8	9		11					7	5	12		3	10				32
1		2*	4	6	3		8	9	12	11		10				5	7							33
1		2		6	3		8	9				10			4	5	7			12	11*			34
1		2	4	6	3		8	9		11		10				5	7							35
		2	4	6	3		8	9		11		10				5	7						1	36
		2	4	6	3		8	9	12	11		10				5	7*						1	37
1		2	4	6	3		8	9	7	11		10				5								38
1		2	4	6	3		8	9	7*	11		10				5	12							39
1		2	4	6	3		8	9	12	11*		10				5	7							40
1		2	4	6	3		8	9*	12	11		10				5	7							41
1		2	4	6			8	9*	12	11		10				5	7			3				42
40	1	36	41	42	35	11	40	28	25	35	10	35	7	2	6	35	21	3	1	4	1	1	2	
						4			4	9		2	1		1		3	1	1		1			
			10	3	2		6	7	5	3		20				1	2	2		4				

29

1976-77

#	Month	Date		Opponent	Result	Score	Scorers	Attendance
1	Aug	21	(a)	Ipswich T	L	1-3	Jones	28,490
2		25	(h)	Newcastle U	L	0-2		24,022
3		28	(h)	Middlesbrough	D	0-0		21,721
4	Sep	4	(a)	Manchester U	W	3-2	Coates, Pratt, Moores	60,723
5		11	(h)	Leeds U	W	1-0	Jones	34,725
6		18	(a)	Liverpool	L	0-2		47,421
7		25	(h)	Norwich C	D	1-1	Hoddle	22,440
8	Oct	2	(a)	West Brom A	L	2-4	Jones, Taylor	23,461
9		16	(a)	Derby Co	L	2-8	Osgood (pen), Perryman	24,216
10		20	(h)	Birmingham C	W	1-0	Osgood (pen)	20,193
11		23	(h)	Coventry C	L	0-1		21,877
12		30	(h)	Everton	D	3-3	McAllister, Osgood (pen), Pratt	26,047
13	Nov	6	(a)	West Ham U	L	3-5	Hoddle, Osgood (pen), Duncan	28,997
14		13	(h)	Bristol C	L	0-1		28,795
15		20	(a)	Sunderland	L	1-2	Moores	30,325
16		27	(h)	Stoke C	W	2-0	Osgood 2 (1 pen)	22,500
17	Dec	11	(h)	Manchester C	D	2-2	Taylor 2	24,608
18		18	(a)	Leicester C	L	1-2	Coates	16,397
19		2	(h)	Arsenal	D	2-2	Young, Duncan	47,751
20	Jan	1	(h)	West Ham U	W	2-1	Osgood (pen), Duncan	44,972
21		11	(a)	Queen's Park R	L	1-2	Duncan	24,266
22		22	(h)	Ipswich T	W	1-0	Taylor	35,126
23	Feb	5	(a)	Middlesbrough	L	0-2		21,231
24		12	(h)	Manchester U	L	1-3	Jones	16,956
25		19	(a)	Leeds U	L	1-2	Armstrong	26,858
26		26	(a)	Newcastle U	L	0-2		30,236
27	Mar	5	(a)	Norwich C	W	3-1	Pratt, Armstrong, Taylor	22,949
28		9	(h)	Liverpool	W	1-0	Coates	32,098
29		12	(h)	West Brom A	L	0-2		28,834
30		19	(a)	Birmingham C	W	2-1	Jones, Hoddle	23,398
31		23	(h)	Derby Co	D	0-0		27,359
32		26	(a)	Everton	L	0-4		32,549
33	Apr	2	(a)	Coventry C	D	1-1	Taylor	16,210
34		9	(h)	Queen's Park R	W	3-0	Jones 2, Taylor	32,680
35		11	(a)	Arsenal	L	0-1		47,432
36		12	(a)	Bristol C	L	0-1		27,568
37		16	(h)	Sunderland	D	1-1	Jones	34,155
38		20	(a)	Aston Villa	L	1-2	Armstrong	42,047
39		23	(a)	Stoke C	D	0-0		15,644
40		30	(h)	Aston Villa	W	3-1	Hoddle, Jones, Taylor	30,690
41	May	7	(a)	Manchester C	L	0-5		37,919
42		14	(h)	Leicester C	W	2-0	Pratt, Holmes	26,094

FINAL LEAGUE POSITION: 22nd in Division One

Appearances

Sub. Appearances

Goals

Daines	Naylor	McAllister	Pratt	Young	Osgood	Coates	Perryman	Armstrong	Jones	Neighbour	Conn	Hoddle	Moores	Jennings	Stead	Taylor	Keeley	McNab	Duncan	Gorman	Holmes	No.
1	2	3	4	5	6	7	8	9	10	11												1
1	2	3	4	5	6	7*	8	9	10	11	12											2
1	2	3		5	6	7	8	9	10	11		4										3
1	2	3	12	5	6	7*	8		10	11		4	9									4
1	2	3	12	5	6*	7	8		10	11		4	9									5
	2	3		5	6	7	8		10	11		4	9	1								6
	2		5		6		8		10	11	7	4	9	1	3							7
	2		5		6	12	8		10		7	4	9	1	3*	11						8
	2		6	5	3		8		10		7	4	9	1		11						9
		3	7*	5	6		8		10			4	9	1		11	2	12				10
		3		5	6	7	8		10			4	9*	1		11	2	12				11
	2	3	7	5	6		8		10			4		1		11		12	9*			12
1	2	3	7	5	6	12	8		10			4				11*			9			13
	2		10	5	6		8				7	4		1		11			9	3		14
	2		10	5	6		8				7	4	9	1		11				3		15
	2			5	6	10	8				7	4	9	1		11				3		16
	2			5	6	10	8				7	4	9	1		11				3		17
	2		12	5	6	10	8				7*	4	9	1		11				3		18
	2		12	5	6	10	8				7	4*		1		11			9	3		19
	2			5	6	10	8				7	4		1		11			9	3		20
	2		12	5	6	10*	8				7	4		1		11			9	3		21
	2				6		8		7			4		1		11	5	10	9	3		22
1	2				6		8		7			4				11	5	10	9	3		23
	2				6		8		7			4		1		11	5	10	9	3		24
	2		11	5	6	12	8	9	7			4*		1				10		3		25
1	2		4		5	6	10	8	9			7				11				3		26
1	2		4		6	10	7	9	8			5				11				3		27
1	2	12	4		5	10	8	9	7			6				11				3*		28
1	2		4		5	10	6	8*	9			7				11	12				3	29
1	2		4		5	10	6	9	7			8				11					3	30
1	2		4		5	10	6	9	7			8				11					3	31
1	2		4		5	10	6	9	7			8				11					3	32
1	2		4		5	10	6	9	7			8				11					3	33
1	2		4		5	10	6	9	7			8				11					3	34
1	2		4		5	10	6	9	7			8				11					3	35
1	2		4		5	6	9	7	8							11	12	10			3*	36
1	2		4		5	10	6	9	7			8			3	11						37
	2		4		5	10	6	12	7			8	9	1	3	11*						38
	2		4		5	10	6	11	8			9		1	3						7	39
	2		4		5	10	6	11	7			8	9*	1	3	12						40
	2		4		5	10	6	9	7			8	12	1	3	11*						41
	2		4		5	6	11	8	9			7		1	3						10	42
19	40	10	30	19	42	28	42	20	31	7	12	39	16	23	8	31	5	6	9	15	10	
	2		4		3		1				1		1			1	1	4				
		1	4	1	7	3	1	3	9			4	2			8			4	1		

1977-78

#	Month	Date		Opponent	Result	Score	Scorers	Attendance
1	Aug	20	(h)	Sheffield U	W	4-2	Osgood 2 (2 pens), Duncan, Jones	27,673
2		24	(a)	Blackburn R	D	0-0		9,540
3		27	(h)	Notts Co	W	2-1	Duncan 2	25,839
4	Sep	3	(a)	Cardiff C	D	0-0		8,880
5		10	(h)	Fulham	W	1-0	Jones	31,939
6		17	(a)	Blackpool	W	2-0	Hoddle, Duncan	16,910
7		24	(h)	Luton T	W	2-0	Osgood (pen), Jones	32,814
8	Oct	1	(a)	Orient	D	1-1	Taylor	24,131
9		4	(a)	Hull C	L	0-2		10,966
10		8	(h)	Oldham A	W	5-1	Duncan 2, Robinson, Taylor 2	24,636
11		15	(a)	Charlton A	L	1-4	Taylor	30,706
12		22	(h)	Bristol R	W	9-0	Hoddle, Moores 2, Lee 4, Taylor	26,571
13		29	(a)	Stoke C	W	3-1	Pratt, Armstrong 2	21,012
14	Nov	5	(h)	Burnley	W	3-0	Hoddle, McNab, Taylor	30,634
15		12	(a)	Crystal Palace	W	2-1	Moores, Duncan	40,522
16		19	(h)	Brighton & HA	D	0-0		48,613
17		26	(a)	Bolton W	L	0-1		34,290
18	Dec	3	(h)	Southampton	D	0-0		37,873
19		10	(a)	Sunderland	W	2-1	Duncan 2	31,960
20		17	(h)	Crystal Palace	D	2-2	Hoddle 2	34,211
21		26	(a)	Millwall	W	3-1	Duncan, Lee, Taylor	14,644
22		27	(h)	Mansfield T	D	1-1	Duncan	36,288
23		31	(h)	Blackburn R	W	4-6	Hoddle, Pratt, Lee 2	30,520
24	Jan	2	(a)	Sheffield U	D	2-2	Duncan, Taylor	31,207
25		14	(a)	Notts Co	D	3-3	Pratt 2, Lee	15,709
26		21	(h)	Cardiff C	W	2-1	Duncan 2	29,104
27	Feb	4	(a)	Fulham	D	1-1	Taylor	24,763
28		11	(h)	Blackpool	D	2-2	McAllister, Pratt	28,707
29		22	(a)	Luton T	W	4-1	Hoddle 2, McAllister, Duncan	17,024
30		25	(h)	Orient	D	1-1	Lee	32,869
31	Mar	4	(a)	Oldham A	D	1-1	McNab	14,122
32		11	(h)	Charlton A	W	2-1	Hoddle (pen), Pratt	34,511
33		18	(a)	Bristol R	W	3-2	Pratt, McNab, Jones	17,708
34		22	(h)	Stoke C	W	3-1	McAllister, Lee 2	30,646
35		25	(a)	Mansfield T	D	3-3	Hoddle 2 (1 pen), Jones	12,144
36		27	(h)	Millwall	D	3-3	Hoddle, Jones 2	33,074
37	Apr	1	(a)	Burnley	L	1-2	Taylor	16,916
38		8	(h)	Bolton W	W	1-0	McAllister	50,097
39		15	(a)	Brighton & HA	L	1-3	Jones	32,647
40		22	(h)	Sunderland	L	2-3	Duncan, Taylor	38,220
41		26	(h)	Hull C	W	1-0	Perryman	36,913
42		29	(a)	Southampton	D	0-0		28,846

FINAL LEAGUE POSITION: 3rd in Division Two

Appearances

Sub. Appearances

Goals

Daines	Naylor	Holmes	Hoddle	Osgood	Perryman	Pratt	McNab	Duncan	Jones	Taylor	Coates	Armstrong	Robinson	McAllister	Moores	Stead	Lee	
1	2	3	4	5	6	7	8	9	10	11								1
1	2	3		5	6	7	8	9	10	11	4							2
1	2	3	4	5	6	7	8	9	10	11								3
1	2	3	4	5	6	7	8	9	10	11								4
1	2	3	4	5	6	7	8	9	10	11								5
1	2	3	4	5	6	7	8	9	10	11								6
1	2	3	4	5	6	7	8	9*	10	11		12						7
1	2	3	4	5	6	7	8			11		9	10					8
1	2	3	4	5	6	7*	8			11	12	9	10					9
1	2	3	4	5	6	7	8	9		11	12		10*					10
1	2	3	4		6	7	8			11		10*	5	9	12			11
1	2	3	4		6	7	8			11			5	9			10	12
1	2	3	4		6	7	8			11		10	5	9				13
1	2	3	4		6	7	8			11		12	5*	9			10	14
1	2	3	4	5	6	7	8*	10		11		12		9				15
1	2	3	4	5	6	7	8	10*		11				9	12			16
1	2	3	4	5	6	7	8	10		11				9				17
1	2		4	5*	6	7	8	10		11		12		3			9	18
1	2	3*	4	5	6	7	8	9		11		12					10	19
1	2		4	5	6	7	8	9		11				3			10	20
1	2		4	5	6	7	8	9		11				3			10	21
1	2		4	5	6	7	8	9	10	11				3				22
1	2	3	4		6	7	8	9*		11		12		5			10	23
1	2	3	4		6	7	8	9		11		12		5*			10	24
1	2	3	4		6	7	8	9				11		5			10	25
1	2	3	4		6	7	8	9		11				5			10	26
1	2	3	4		6	7	8	9		11				5			10	27
1	2	3	4		6	7	8	9		11				5			10	28
1	2	3	4		6	7	8	9		11				5*	12		10	29
1	2	3	4		6	7	8	9		11		5					10	30
1	2	3	4		6	7	8		9	11		5					10	31
1	2	3	4		6	7	8		9	11				5			10	32
1	2*	3	4		6	7	8		9	11				5	12		10	33
1		3	4		6	7	8		9	11				5		2	10	34
1		3	4		6	7	8		9	11				5		2	10	35
1		3	4		6	7	8		9	11		2		5			10	36
1		3	4		6	7	8		9	11		2		5			10	37
1		3	4		6	7	8		9	11		2		5	12		10*	38
1	2	3	4		6	7	8		9	11		12		5			10*	39
1	2	3	4		6	7*	8	10	9	11		5					12	40
1	2	3	4		6	7	8	10	9	11				5				41
1	2	3	4		6	7	8	10*	9	11		12		5				42
42	37	38	41	18	42	42	42	27	20	41	1	10	4	25	7	2	23	
											2	9		3	1	2		
		12	3	1	7	3	16	8	11			2	1	4	4		11	

1978-79

1	Aug	19	(a)	Nottingham F	D	1-1	Villa	41,223
2		23	(h)	Aston Villa	L	1-4	Hoddle (pen)	47,892
3		26	(h)	Chelsea	D	2-2	Armstrong, Duncan	40,632
4	Sep	2	(a)	Liverpool	L	0-7		50,705
5		9	(h)	Bristol C	W	1-0	Rodgers (og)	34,035
6		16	(a)	Leeds U	W	2-1	Lee, Taylor	36,062
7		23	(a)	Manchester C	L	0-2		43,471
8		30	(h)	Coventry C	D	1-1	Hoddle	35,806
9	Oct	7	(a)	West Brom A	W	1-0	Taylor	33,068
10		14	(h)	Birmingham C	W	1-0	Ainscow (og)	41,236
11		21	(a)	Derby Co	D	2-2	McAllister, Taylor	26,181
12		28	(h)	Bolton W	W	2-0	Pratt, Lee	37,337
13	Nov	4	(a)	Norwich C	D	2-2	Lee, Taylor	27,033
14		11	(h)	Nottingham F	L	1-3	Pratt	50,543
15		18	(a)	Chelsea	W	3-1	Lee 2, Hoddle	42,323
16		22	(h)	Liverpool	D	0-0		50,393
17		25	(h)	Wolverhampton W	W	1-0	Taylor	35,430
18	Dec	9	(h)	Ipswich T	W	1-0	Pratt	33,882
19		16	(a)	Manchester U	L	0-2		52,026
20		23	(h)	Arsenal	L	0-5		42,273
21		26	(a)	Queen's Park R	D	2-2	Lee, Taylor (pen)	24,845
22		30	(a)	Everton	D	1-1	Taylor	44,572
23	Jan	13	(a)	Bristol C	D	0-0		29,122
24		20	(h)	Leeds U	L	1-2	Hoddle	36,838
25	Feb	3	(h)	Manchester C	L	0-3		32,037
26		10	(a)	Coventry C	W	3-1	Lee, Taylor 2	25,071
27		24	(a)	Birmingham C	L	0-1		20,980
28	Mar	3	(h)	Derby Co	W	2-0	Ardiles 2	28,089
29		17	(h)	Norwich C	D	0-0		24,982
30		24	(a)	Aston Villa	W	3-2	Jones, Hoddle 2	35,486
31		28	(h)	Southampton	D	0-0		23,570
32		31	(a)	Middlesbrough	L	0-1		19,172
33	Apr	3	(a)	Wolverhampton W	L	2-3	Jones 2	19,819
34		7	(h)	Middlesbrough	L	1-2	Taylor (pen)	21,580
35		10	(a)	Arsenal	L	0-1		53,896
36		14	(h)	Queen's Park R	D	1-1	Perryman	28,854
37		16	(a)	Southampton	D	3-3	Pratt, Jones, Taylor	22,096
38		21	(h)	Manchester U	D	1-1	Jones	36,665
39		28	(a)	Ipswich T	L	1-2	Hoddle (pen)	28,179
40	May	5	(h)	Everton	D	1-1	Ardiles	26,077
41		8	(a)	Bolton W	W	3-1	Holmes, Falco, Villa	17,879
42		14	(h)	West Brom A	W	1-0	Villa	24,789

FINAL LEAGUE POSITION: 11th in Division One

Appearances

Sub. Appearances

Goals

Daines	McAllister	Gorman	Hoddle	Lacy	Perryman	Villa	Ardiles	Armstrong	Moores	Taylor	Pratt	Duncan	McNab	Naylor	Holmes	Lee	Kendall	Jones	Aleksic	Galvin	Beavon	Miller	Falco	Smith	No.
1	2	3	4	5	6	7	8	9	10	11*	12														1
1	2	3	4	5	6	7	8	9	10	11															2
1	2	3	4	5	6	7	8	9				10	11												3
1	2		4	5	6	7	8			9		10	11	3											4
1	2	3		5	6	7	8			11	10				4	9									5
1	2	3		5	6	7*	8	12		11	10				4	9									6
1	2	3		5	6*	7	8	12		11	10				4	9									7
1	2	3	12	5	6		8	7*		11	10				4	9									8
1	2	3	7		6		8	5		11	10				4	9									9
1		3	10	5	6		8			11	7			2	4	9									10
1		3	10	5	6		8			11	7			2	4	9									11
1		3	10*	5	6	12	8			11	7			2	4	9									12
		3	10	5	6	12	8*			11	7			2	4	9	1								3
		3	10	5	6	12	8*			11	7			2	4	9	1								14
	2	3	10	5	6		8			11	7				4	9	1								15
	2	3	10*	5	6	12	8			11	7				4	9	1								16
	2	3	10*	5	6	12	8			11	7				4	9	1								17
	2	3	10	5	6		8			11	7				4	9	1								18
	2	3	10	5	6	12	8			11	7				4*	9	1								19
		3	10	5	6		8			11	7*			2	4	9	1	12							20
		3		5	6	4	8			11	7			2		9	1	10							21
		3		5	6	4	8			11	7			2		9	1	10							22
		3		5	6	4	8			11	7				2	9	1	10							23
	2		4	5	6		8			11	7				3	9		10	1						24
	2		4	5	6		8	9		11					3		1					7	10		25
		10	4	5	6		8*	12		11	7			2	3	9	1								26
			4	5	6	9	8			11	7			2	3		1	10							27
		9	4	5	6	11	8				7			2	3		1	10							28
		3	10	5	6	11	8*			12	7			2	4	9	1								29
		3	10	5	6	11	8				7			2	4		1	9							30
		3	10	5	6	11	8				7			2	4		1	9							31
		3	10	5	6	11	8*				7			2	4	12	1	9							32
		3	10	5	6	11	8				7			2	4		1	9							33
		3	10		6	11	8	7		5				2	4		1	9							34
1		3	10		6	11	8				7			2	4			9				5			35
1		3	10		6	11	8				7			2	4			9				5			36
		3			6	8	10			11	7			2	4		1	9				5			37
		3	8	5	6	7	10			11	2						1	9				4			38
		3	10	5	6	11	8				7			2	9		1	4							39
		3	10		6	11	8	7		5				2	9		1	4							40
		3*	10		6	11	8	7		5				2			1	4	9				12		41
	5		10	4	6	11	8	7						2			1	9						3	42
14	28	15	34	35	42	26	38	7	2	32	37	2	2	22	33	26	23	18	5	1	1	7	1	1	
			1		6		3			1	1						1	1					1		
	1		7	1	3	3	1			11	4	1			1	7		5				1			

1979-80

1	Aug	18	(h)	Middlesbrough	L	1-3	Hoddle	32,743
2		22	(a)	Norwich C	L	0-4		16,647
3		25	(a)	Stoke C	L	1-3	Perryman	22,832
4	Sep	1	(h)	Manchester C	W	2-1	Jones, Hoddle	30,901
5		8	(h)	Brighton & HA	W	2-1	Armstrong, Hoddle (pen)	34,107
6		15	(a)	Southampton	L	2-5	Jones, Hoddle	22,573
7		22	(h)	West Brom A	D	1-1	Hoddle (pen)	29,914
8		29	(a)	Coventry C	D	1-1	Jones	20,085
9	Oct	6	(a)	Crystal Palace	D	1-1	Villa	45,274
10		10	(h)	Norwich C	W	3-2	Hoddle 2, Villa	26,488
11		13	(h)	Derby Co	W	1-0	Armstrong	33,269
12		20	(a)	Leeds U	W	2-1	Jones, Armstrong	25,203
13		27	(h)	Nottingham F	W	1-0	Hoddle	49,038
14	Nov	3	(a)	Middlesbrough	D	0-0		19,557
15		10	(h)	Bolton W	W	2-0	Yorath, Hoddle (pen)	33,155
16		17	(a)	Liverpool	L	1-2	Jones	51,092
17		24	(a)	Everton	D	1-1	Jones	31,079
18	Dec	1	(h)	Manchester C	L	1-2	Hoddle	51,389
19		8	(a)	Bristol C	W	3-1	Miller, Hoddle 2 (1 pen)	25,090
20		15	(h)	Aston Villa	L	1-2	Ardiles	30,555
21		21	(a)	Ipswich T	L	1-3	McAllister	18,945
22		26	(a)	Arsenal	L	0-1		44,560
23		29	(h)	Stoke C	W	1-0	Pratt	28,810
24	Jan	12	(a)	Manchester C	D	1-1	Hoddle	34,837
25		19	(a)	Brighton & HA	W	2-0	Hughton, Villa	29,406
26	Feb	2	(h)	Southampton	D	0-0		37,155
27		9	(a)	West Brom A	L	1-2	Hoddle	26,319
28		23	(a)	Derby Co	L	1-2	Galvin	21,183
29		27	(h)	Coventry C	W	4-3	Falco, Hoddle 3 (2 pen)	22,536
30	Mar	1	(h)	Leeds U	W	2-1	Falco, Hoddle	35,331
31		11	(a)	Nottingham F	L	0-4		25,633
32		15	(h)	Crystal Palace	D	0-0		28,419
33		22	(a)	Bolton W	L	1-2	Jones	14,474
34		29	(h)	Liverpool	W	2-0	Pratt, Hoddle (pen)	31,114
35	Apr	2	(h)	Ipswich T	L	0-2		26,423
36		5	(a)	Wolverhampton W	W	2-1	Jones, Galvin	30,713
37		7	(h)	Arsenal	L	1-2	Jones	41,365
38		12	(a)	Manchester U	L	1-4	Ardiles	53,151
39		19	(h)	Everton	W	3-0	Miller, Ardiles, Galvin	25,245
40		23	(h)	Wolverhampton W	D	2-2	Armstrong, Galvin	19,753
41		26	(a)	Aston Villa	L	0-1		29,549
42	May	3	(h)	Bristol C	D	0-0		23,585

FINAL LEAGUE POSITION: 14th in Division One

Appearances

Sub. Appearances

Goals

.

Daines	Lee	Smith	Yorath	Lacy	Perryman	Pratt	Ardiles	Falco	Hoddle	Villa	Jones	McAllister	Hughton	Miller	Southey	Armstrong	Beavon	Aleksic	Galvin	Gibson	Taylor	Naylor	Kendall	Hazard	#
1	2	3	4	5	6	7*	8	9	10	11	12														1
1	2	3	4	5	6		8	7	10	11	9														2
1	2	3	4	5	6	7	8	9*	10		11	12													3
1	11		4		6	7	8*	12	10		9	2	3	5											4
1	11		4		6	7*			10		8	2		5	3	9	12								5
1			4	5	6	7			10	3	8	2				9	11								6
1			4		6		7		10	11	8	3	2	5		9									7
1			4		6		7		10	11	8	3	2	5		9									8
1			4		6	12	7*		10	11	8	3	2	5		9									9
1			4*		6	12	7		10	11	8	3	2	5		9									10
1	12				6	4	7		10	11	8	3	2	5		9*									11
1*			4		6	12	7		10	11	8	3	2	5		9									12
	12	3	4		6		7		10	11	8	5	2			9*		1							13
		5	4		6		7		10	11	8	3	2			9		1							14
		5	4		6		7		10	11	8	3	2			9		1							15
		5	4		6		7		10	11	8	3	2			9		1							16
		5	4		6		7		10	11	8	3	2			9		1							17
		5			6	4	7		10	11	8	3	2			9		1							18
1	9	5			6	4	7		10	11	8		2	3											19
1	9	5			6	4	7		10	11	8		2	3											20
1	9		4		6		7		10	11	8	5	2	3											21
		5	4		6	11	7		10		8	3	2			9*		1	12						22
		3	4		6	11	7		10		8	5	2					1	12	9*					23
1			4		6	12	7		10	11	8*	3	2	5		9									24
1			4		6	12	7		10	11		5	2	3		9					8*				25
1			4			8	7		10			5	2	3		9					11	6			26
1			4				7		10	11	8	5	2	3		9						6			27
					6	4	7	8	10			5	2	3		9	11*		12				1		28
		11			6	4	7	8	10			5	2	3		9							1		29
1		11			6		7	8	10	4		5	2	3		9									30
1		4*			6		7		10		8	5	2	3		9					11	12			31
1		4			6		7		10		8	5		3		9					11	2			32
1					6		7		10		8	5		3	4	9					11	2			33
1		4			6	9	7		10		8	5		3		12					11*	2			34
1		4			6	9	7		10		8	5		3							11	2			35
1		2			6	11	7		10		8	5		3	4				9						36
1		4			6	9	7		10		8	5		3	2				11						37
1		4			6	9	7		10		8	5		3	2	12			11*						38
1					6		7		10		8	5		3	2	9			11		12		4*		39
1					6		7				8*	5		3	2	9			11		12		10		40
1					6	4	7	12	10		8	3	2	5		11*			9						41
1					6		7	9	10		8	5		3	2				11				4		42
32	8	14	33	4	40	19	40	7	41	22	36	35	39	27	1	28	2	8	7	1	7	6	2	3	
	2					5		2				1	1			2	1		3		2	1			
			1		1	2	3	2	19	3	9	1	1	2		4			4						

1980-81

1	Aug	16	(h)	Nottingham F	W	2-0	Hoddle (pen), Crooks	43,398
2		19	(a)	Crystal Palace	W	4-3	Archibald, Hoddle, Crooks 2	27,841
3		23	(h)	Brighton & HA	D	2-2	Hoddle, Crooks	39,763
4		30	(a)	Arsenal	L	0-2		54,045
5	Sep	6	(h)	Manchester U	D	0-0		40,995
6		13	(a)	Leeds U	D	0-0		21,947
7		20	(h)	Sunderland	D	0-0		32,030
8		27	(a)	Leicester C	L	1-2	Villa	22,616
9	Oct	4	(a)	Stoke C	W	3-2	Hughton, Archibald, Taylor (pen)	18,614
10		11	(h)	Middlesbrough	W	3-2	Archibald, Villa, Crooks	27,380
11		18	(a)	Aston Villa	L	0-3		30,940
12		22	(a)	Manchester C	L	1-3	Hoddle	28,788
13		25	(h)	Coventry C	W	4-1	Archibald 2, Hoddle 2	25,484
14	Nov	1	(a)	Everton	D	2-2	Archibald 2	26,223
15		8	(h)	Wolverhampton W	D	2-2	Hoddle (pen), Crooks	29,244
16		12	(h)	Crystal Palace	W	4-2	Archibald, Crooks 3	25,777
17		15	(a)	Nottingham F	W	3-0	Ardiles, Archibald 2	25,400
18		22	(a)	Birmingham C	L	1-2	Ardiles	24,817
19		29	(h)	West Brom A	L	2-3	Lacy, Perryman	27,372
20	Dec	6	(a)	Liverpool	L	1-2	Archibald	39,545
21		13	(h)	Manchester C	W	2-1	Archibald, Hoddle	23,883
22		17	(h)	Ipswich T	W	5-3	Perryman, Ardiles, Archibald, Hoddle, Crooks	22,741
23		20	(a)	Middlesbrough	L	1-4	Lacy	15,990
24		26	(h)	Southampton	D	4-4	Brooke 2, Archibald, Crooks	28,792
25		27	(a)	Norwich C	D	2-2	Archibald, Hoddle	23,145
26	Jan	10	(h)	Birmingham C	W	1-0	Crooks	24,909
27		17	(h)	Arsenal	W	2-0	Archibald 2	32,944
28		31	(a)	Brighton & HA	W	2-0	Ardiles, Crooks	23,610
29	Feb	7	(h)	Leeds U	D	1-1	Archibald	32,372
30		17	(a)	Manchester U	D	0-0		40,642
31		21	(h)	Leicester C	L	1-2	Archibald	27,326
32		28	(a)	Sunderland	D	1-1	Crooks	22,382
33	Mar	11	(h)	Stoke C	D	2-2	Ardiles, Brooke	28,742
34		14	(a)	Ipswich T	L	0-3		32,044
35		21	(h)	Aston Villa	W	2-0	Archibald, Crooks	35,091
36		28	(a)	Coventry C	W	1-0	Roberts (og)	18,654
37	Apr	4	(h)	Everton	D	2-2	Galvin, Crooks	27,208
38		18	(h)	Norwich C	L	2-3	Miller, Hoddle (pen)	34,413
39		20	(a)	Southampton	D	1-1	Miller	23,735
40		25	(h)	Liverpool	D	1-1	Hoddle	35,334
41		30	(a)	Wolverhampton W	L	0-1		18,350
42	May	2	(a)	West Brom A	L	2-4	Smith, Falco	20,549

FINAL LEAGUE POSITION: 10th in Division One

Appearances

Sub. Appearances

Goals

Kendall	Smith	Hughton	Yorath	Lacy	Perryman	Ardiles	Archibald	Villa	Hoddle	Crooks	Armstrong	Taylor	Daines	Roberts	Miller	McAllister	Brooke	Aleksic	O'Reilly	Galvin	Mazzon	Hazard	Falco	No.
1	2	3	4	5	6	7*	8	9	10	11	12													1
1	2	3	4	5	6	7	8	9	10	11														2
1	2	3	4	5	6	7	8	9	10	11														3
1	2*	3	4	5	6	7	8	9	10	11		12												4
	2	3	4	5	6	7*	8	9	10	11		12	1											5
	2	3		5	6	7	8	9	10	11		4	1											6
	2	3		5	6	7	8	9	10	11	12	4*	1											7
	2	3	4	5	6	7	8	9	10	11			1											8
	2	3	4	5	6	7	8	9		11*		10	1	12										9
	2	3	4	5	6	7*	8	9	10	11		12	1											10
	2	3	4*	5	6		8	9	10	11	12	7	1											11
	2	3		5	6	7	8	9	10	11*	12	4	1											12
	2	3		5	6	7	8	9	10	11			1		4									13
	2	3		5	6	7	8	9	10	11			1		4									14
	2	3*		5	6	7	8	9	10	11			1	12	4									15
		3		5	6	7	8	9	10	11			1	12	4	2*								16
		3		5	6	7	8	9	10	11			1		4	2								17
		3		5	6	7	8	9	10	11			1		4	2								18
		3		5	6	7*	8	9	10	11			1		4	2	12							19
		3		5	6	7	8	9	10	11			1	4		2								20
		3	12	5	6	7*	8	9	10	11			1	4		2								21
		3	12	5	6	7	8	9*	10	11			1	4		2								22
		3	12	5	6	7	8	9	10	11				4*		2		1						23
		3*	2	5	6		8	9	10	11				4			7	1	12					24
			4	5	6		8	9*	10	11				2	12		7	1	3					25
				5	6		8		10	11			1	4	3	2	7*			9	12			26
		12	5*	6			8		10	11			1	4	3	2	7			9				27
				5	6	7*	8		10	11			1	4	3	2	12			9				28
				5	6	7	8		10	11*			1	4	3	2	12			9				29
	2			5	6	7	8		10	11			1	4	3					9				30
	2			5	6	7	8		10	11*			1	4	3		12			9				31
12	2				6	7	8*		10	11			1	4	3					9	5			32
	2*				6	7	8		10	11			1	4	3	5	12			9				33
	2				6	7*	8		10	11			1	4	3	5	12			9				34
	2				6	7	8		10	11				4	3		5	1		9				35
12	2				6	7	8		10	11				4	3		5*	1		9				36
	2				6	7	8	12	10	11				4	3		5*	1		9				37
	2				6	7	8		10	11				4	3		5*	1		9		12		38
	2				3	7		6		11*				4	5		12	1		9		10	8	39
	2				6	7	8	5*	10	11				3	4		12	1		9				40
	2				6	7	8						1	4	3*	10	5			9		12	11	41
	2				6				12	5				10*	3	4	7	1		9		8	11	42
4	18	34	11	31	42	36	40	28	38	40	5	28	21	24	18	10	10	1	17	1	2	3		
	2		4				1	1				4	3		3	1	8		1		1	2		
		1	1		2	2	5	20	2	12	16		1		2		3			1		1		

39

1981-82

1	Aug	29	(a)	Middlesbrough	W	3-1	Villa, Hoddle, Falco	20,490
2	Sep	2	(h)	West Ham U	L	0-4		41,208
3		5	(h)	Aston Villa	L	1-3	Villa	31,265
4		12	(a)	Wolverhampton W	W	1-0	Galvin	18,675
5		19	(h)	Everton	W	3-0	Hughton, Roberts, Hoddle (pen)	31,219
6		22	(a)	Swansea C	L	1-2	Hoddle (pen)	22,352
7		26	(a)	Manchester C	W	1-0	Falco	39,085
8	Oct	3	(h)	Nottingham F	W	3-0	Hazard, Falco 2	34,876
9		10	(h)	Stoke C	W	2-0	Ardiles, Crooks	30,520
10		17	(a)	Sunderland	W	2-0	Hazard, Archibald	25,317
11		24	(h)	Brighton & HA	L	0-1		37,294
12		31	(a)	Southampton	W	2-1	Roberts, Corbett	24,131
13	Nov	7	(h)	West Brom A	L	1-2	Crooks	32,436
14		21	(h)	Manchester U	W	3-1	Roberts, Hazard, Archibald	35,534
15		28	(a)	Notts Co	D	2-2	Crooks 2	15,556
16	Dec	5	(h)	Coventry C	L	1-2	Hazard	27,952
17		12	(a)	Leeds U	D	0-0		28,780
18	Jan	27	(h)	Middlesbrough	W	1-0	Crooks	22,819
19		30	(a)	Everton	D	1-1	Villa	30,709
20	Feb	6	(h)	Wolverhampton W	W	6-1	Villa 3, Falco, Hoddle (pen), Crooks	29,960
21		17	(a)	Aston Villa	D	1-1	Crooks	23,877
22		20	(h)	Manchester C	W	2-0	Hoddle 2 (1 pen)	46,181
23		27	(a)	Stoke C	W	2-0	Crooks	20,592
24	Mar	9	(a)	Brighton & HA	W	3-1	Ardiles, Archibald, Crooks	27,082
25		20	(h)	Southampton	W	3-2	Roberts 3	46,827
26		23	(a)	Birmingham C	D	0-0		17,708
27		27	(a)	West Brom A	L	0-1		20,151
28		29	(h)	Arsenal	D	2-2	Hughton, Archibald	40,946
29	Apr	10	(h)	Ipswich T	W	1-0	Hoddle	45,215
30		12	(a)	Arsenal	W	3-1	Hazard, Crooks 2	48,897
31		14	(h)	Sunderland	D	2-2	Galvin, Hoddle	39,898
32		17	(a)	Manchester U	L	0-2		50,724
33		24	(h)	Notts Co	W	3-1	Villa, Archibald, Galvin	38,017
34		28	(h)	Birmingham C	D	1-1	Villa	25,470
35	May	1	(a)	Coventry C	D	0-0		15,408
36		3	(h)	Liverpool	D	2-2	Perryman, Archibald	38,091
37		5	(h)	Swansea C	W	2-1	Brooke 2 (1 pen)	26,348
38		8	(h)	Leeds U	W	2-1	Brooke, Burns (og)	35,020
39		10	(a)	West Ham U	D	2-2	Hoddle (pen), Brooke	27,667
40		12	(a)	Nottingham F	L	0-2		15,273
41		15	(a)	Liverpool	L	1-3	Hoddle	48,122
42		17	(a)	Ipswich T	L	1-2	Crooks	21,202

FINAL LEAGUE POSITION: 4th in Division One

Appearances

Sub. Appearances

Goals

Clemence	Hughton	Miller	Price	Villa	Perryman	Ardiles	Brooke	Galvin	Hoddle	Falco	Roberts	Hazard	Smith	Jones	Lacy	Archibald	Crooks	Corbett	Dick	Gibson	O'Reilly	Crook	Aleksic	Parks	Match
1	2	3	4	5	6	7	8	9	10	11															1
1		3	4*	5	6		8	9	10	11	2	7	12												2
1		3*		5	6	7	8		10	11	2		4	9	12										3
1	2	3		5	6	7	8*	9	10	11	4			12											4
1	2	3		5	6	7		9	10	11	4					8									5
1	2	3		5	6	7		9	10	11	4					8									6
1	2	3		5	6	7		9	10	11	4					8									7
1	2	3			6	7		9	10	11	4	5				8									8
1	2	3	5*		6	7		9	10		4	12				8	11								9
1	2	3			6	7		9	10		4	5*			12	8	11								10
1	2	3			6	7		9	10		4	5				8	11								11
1	2	3			6	7		9	10		4	5				8	11*	12							12
1	2	3	10		6	7*		9			4	5			12	8	11								13
1	2	3			6	7		9	10		4	5				8	11								14
1	2	3			6	7		9	10		4	5				8	11								15
1	2*	3	12		6	7		9	10		4	5				8	11								16
1	2	3	8		6	7		9	10		4	5*			12		11								17
1	2	3		5	6	7		9	10	8	4						11								18
1	2	3	4	5	6	7	12	9	10	8*							11								19
1	2	3	4	5	6	7		9	10	8		12					11*								20
1	2	3	9		6	7			10	8	4*	5				12	11								21
1	2	3	4		6	7			10		12	5				8	11	9*							22
1	2	3	4		6	7*		9	10		12	5				8	11								23
1	2	3	4		6	7		9			10	5				8	11								24
1	2	3	4	11	6			9	10		7	5				8									25
1	2	3		11	6	7		9		10	4	5			12					8*					26
1	2	3	5	11	6	7	12	9	10*		4					8									27
1	2		4	5	6	7		9	10		3	11				8									28
1	2	3	7		6		12	9	10		4	5				8*	11								29
1		3	4	7	6			9	10		2	5	8				11								30
1		3	4	7	6		12	9*	10		2	5	8				11								31
1	2	3*	12	7	6			9	10		4	5				8	11								32
1	2	3		7	6			9	10		4	5				8	11								33
1	2	3		7	6			9			4	10			5	8	11								34
1	2			7	6		11	9*	10		4										3	12			35
	2	3			6				10	9	4*			12	5	8					7	11	1		36
	2	3			6				10	9	4			12	5	8			3		7	11*	1		37
1	2				6		4		10	9	12				5		11	3			7	8*			38
		3	4		6		8		10	9		7			5		11	2*			12			1	39
1	2	3		9	6	7			10	8	4				5		11								40
1	2	3	12	9	6	7			10	8	4	5					11*								41
	2	3	12	9	6	7			10*		4	5				8	11							1	42
38	37	35	18	26	42	26	12	32	34	21	35	26	2	3	7	26	27	3	1	1	4	3	2	2	
			3	1			4				2	2	1	4	5	1	1				1	1			
	2			8	1	2	4	3	10	5	6	5				6	13	1							

41

1982-83

1	Aug	28	(h)	Luton T	D	2-2	Hazard, Mabbutt	35,195
2		31	(a)	Ipswich T	W	2-1	Archibald, Crooks	23,224
3	Sep	4	(a)	Everton	L	1-3	Archibald	30,563
4		8	(h)	Southampton	W	6-0	Brooke (pen), Perryman, Galvin 2, Villa, Crooks	26,579
5		11	(h)	Manchester C	L	1-2	Mabbutt	32,483
6		18	(a)	Sunderland	W	1-0	Brooke	21,137
7		25	(h)	Nottingham F	W	4-1	Mabbutt 2, Crooks 2	30,662
8	Oct	2	(a)	Swansea C	L	0-2		16,381
9		9	(h)	Coventry C	W	4-0	Crooks, Brooke 3 (1 pen)	25,188
10		16	(a)	Norwich C	D	0-0		21,668
11		23	(h)	Notts Co	W	4-2	Brooke, Mabbutt, Crooks 2	26,183
12		30	(a)	Aston Villa	L	0-4		25,992
13	Nov	6	(h)	Watford	L	0-1		42,634
14		13	(a)	Manchester U	L	0-1		47,869
15		20	(h)	West Ham U	W	2-1	Archibald 2	41,960
16		27	(a)	Liverpool	L	0-3		40,691
17	Dec	4	(h)	West Brom A	D	1-1	Wile (og)	26,608
18		11	(a)	Stoke C	L	0-2		15,849
19		18	(h)	Birmingham C	W	2-1	Mabbutt 2	20,946
20		27	(a)	Arsenal	L	0-2		51,497
21		28	(h)	Brighton & HA	W	2-0	Villa, Hughton	23,994
22	Jan	1	(a)	West Ham U	L	0-3		33,383
23		3	(h)	Everton	W	2-1	Gibson 2	28,455
24		15	(a)	Luton T	D	1-1	Hoddle	21,231
25		22	(h)	Sunderland	D	1-1	Gibson	25,250
26	Feb	5	(a)	Manchester C	D	2-2	Gibson, Brooke (pen)	26,357
27		12	(h)	Swansea C	W	1-0	Crooks	24,632
28		16	(h)	Norwich C	D	0-0		23,342
29	Mar	5	(a)	Notts Co	L	0-3		11,841
30		12	(a)	Coventry C	D	1-1	Miller	11,027
31		19	(a)	Watford	W	1-0	Falco	27,373
32		23	(h)	Aston Villa	W	2-0	Falco 2	22,455
33	Apr	2	(a)	Brighton & HA	L	1-2	Roberts	20,341
34		4	(h)	Arsenal	W	5-0	Hughton 2, Brazil, Falco 2	43,642
35		9	(a)	Nottingham F	D	2-2	Mabbutt, Brazil	18,265
36		16	(h)	Ipswich T	W	3-1	Mabbutt, Brazil 2	30,587
37		23	(a)	West Brom A	W	1-0	Archibald	14,879
38		30	(h)	Liverpool	W	2-0	Archibald 2	44,907
39	May	3	(a)	Southampton	W	2-1	Mabbutt, Brazil	21,602
40		7	(a)	Birmingham C	L	0-2		18,947
41		11	(h)	Manchester U	W	2-0	Roberts, Archibald	32,803
42		14	(h)	Stoke C	W	4-1	Brazil, Archibald 3	33,691

FINAL LEAGUE POSITION: 4th in Division One

Appearances

Sub. Appearances

Goals

Clemence	Hughton	Miller	Lacy	Hazard	Perryman	Mabbutt	Archibald	Galvin	Hoddle	Crooks	Brooke	Price	Villa	Roberts	Falco	Crook	O'Reilly	Parks	Corbett	Mazzon	Webster	Gibson	Dick	Ardiles	Brazil	#
1	2	3	4	5	6	7	8*	9	10	11	12															1
1	2	3	4		6	7	8	9	10	11	5															2
1	2	3*	4	12	6	7	8	9	10	11	5															3
1	2		4	7	6		8	9	10*	11	5	3	12													4
1			4	7*	6	2	8	9		11	5	3	10	12												5
1	2	4			6	7	8	9		11	5	3	10													6
1	2	4		8*	6	7				11	5	3	10	9	12											7
1	2	3		9	6	7	8			11	5*	4	10		12											8
	2	4	3	9		7	8*			11	5		10	12			6	1								9
1		4	3	9		7	8			11	5	2	10				6									10
1		4	5	6				9		11	7	2	10*	8	12		3									11
1	3	4	5		6			9		11	7	2	10	8												12
1	2	3	5	12	6	2	8		10	11	4	9*														13
1	2	3	5		6	7	8		10	11	9						4									14
1	2		5	6*	7	8			10	11	12	3	9				4									15
1	2		5*	6	10	8	9			11		3	7	12			4									16
1	2				7	8	9	10	11			3	5	6			4									17
1	2	4			7	8	9	10	11*			3	5	6					12							18
1	2	3	8	6	7			9	10	11	12		5*	4												19
1	2		5	6	7	8		9*	10	11	12			4			3									20
1	2		5	6		8			10	11	7	9	4*	12			3									21
1	2			6		8			10	11	9	4	5	7			3									22
1	2			6		8			10		7	4	5				3					9	11			23
1	2			6	11	8					12	5	10	4			3					9*	7			24
1	2	3		6	11	8			10			5	4									9	7			25
1	2	3		6		8				11	10	5	4		12							9		7*		26
1	2*	3		6		8		7		11	10	4	5		12							9				27
1	2	3	5*	6		8		7		11			4	10	12							9				28
1	2	3		6		8		7		11		4	5*	12	10							9				29
1	2	5			6	8					7		4	10	11*		3				12	9				30
1	2	5			6	7	8						4	9			3					11			10	31
1	2	5			6	7		11	10*				4	9			3					12			8	32
1	2	5	12			7	8			11			4	9			3					6*			10	33
1	2	5			7	8	9						4	11			3					6			10	34
1	2	5	12		7	8	9						4	11			3*					6			10	35
1	2	5			6	7	8				12		4	11			3*					9			10	36
1	2	5			6	7	8	9	10				4				3					12			11*	37
1	2	5			6	7	8	9	10				4				3								11	38
1	2	5			6	7	8	9	10				4				3								11	39
1	2	5			7	8	9	10					4	12			3					6*			11	40
1		5	2		6	7	8	9	10				4				3								11	41
1	2	5	4		6	7	8	9	10					12			3*								11	42
41	38	23	22	15	32	38	31	26	22	26	19	16	21	20	11	1	25	1		2	1	14	2	2	12	
	3	1			3	1					2		4	1	4	5	3	1	1			1			2	
	3	1		1	1		10	11	2	1	8	7		2	2		5					4			6	

43

1983-84

								Attendance
1	Aug	27	(a)	Ipswich T	L	1-3	Archibald	26,562
2		29	(h)	Coventry C	D	1-1	Hoddle (pen)	35,454
3	Sep	3	(h)	West Ham U	L	0-2		38,042
4		7	(a)	West Brom A	D	1-1	Roberts	14,830
5		10	(a)	Leicester C	W	3-0	Stevens, Mabbutt, Crooks	15,886
6		17	(h)	Everton	L	1-2	Falco	29,125
7		24	(a)	Watford	W	3-2	Hughton, Hoddle, Archibald	21,056
8	Oct	2	(h)	Nottingham F	W	2-1	Stevens, Archibald	30,596
9		15	(a)	Wolverhampton W	W	3-2	Archibald 2, Falco	12,523
10		22	(h)	Birmingham C	W	1-0	Archibald	18,937
11		29	(h)	Notts Co	W	1-0	Archibald	29,198
12	Nov	5	(a)	Stoke C	D	1-1	Falco	14,726
13		12	(h)	Liverpool	D	2-2	Archibald, Hoddle (pen)	44,348
14		19	(a)	Luton T	W	4-2	Dick, Archibald 2, Cooke	17,275
15		26	(h)	Queen's Park R	W	3-2	Archibald, Falco 2	38,789
16	Dec	3	(a)	Norwich C	L	1-2	Dick	21,987
17		10	(h)	Southampton	D	0-0		29,711
18		16	(a)	Manchester U	L	2-4	Brazil, Falco	33,616
19		26	(h)	Arsenal	L	2-4	Roberts, Archibald	38,756
20		27	(a)	Aston Villa	D	0-0		30,125
21		31	(a)	West Ham U	L	1-4	Stevens	30,939
22	Jan	2	(h)	Watford	L	2-3	Hughton, Hoddle (pen)	32,495
23		14	(h)	Ipswich T	W	2-0	Roberts, Falco	25,832
24		21	(a)	Everton	L	1-2	Archibald	17,990
25	Feb	4	(a)	Nottingham F	D	2-2	Hughton, Falco	21,482
26		8	(h)	Sunderland	W	3-0	Perryman, Archibald 2	19,327
27		11	(a)	Leicester C	W	3-2	Archibald, Falco, Galvin	28,410
28		21	(a)	Notts Co	D	0-0		7,943
29		25	(h)	Birmingham C	L	0-1		23,564
30	Mar	3	(h)	Stoke C	W	1-0	Falco (pen)	18,271
31		10	(a)	Liverpool	L	1-3	Stevens	36,718
32		17	(h)	West Brom A	L	0-1		22,385
33		24	(a)	Coventry C	W	4-2	Roberts, Hazard, Brazil 2 (1 pen)	12,847
34		31	(h)	Wolverhampton W	W	1-0	Hazard	19,296
35	Apr	7	(a)	Sunderland	D	1-1	Falco	15,433
36		14	(h)	Luton T	W	2-1	Roberts, Falco	25,390
37		18	(h)	Aston Villa	W	2-1	Roberts (pen), Mabbutt	18,668
38		21	(a)	Arsenal	L	2-3	Archibald 2	48,831
39		28	(a)	Queen's Park R	L	1-2	Archibald	24,937
40	May	5	(h)	Norwich C	W	2-0	Archibald, Falco	18,874
41		7	(a)	Southampton	L	0-5		21,141
42		12	(h)	Manchester U	D	1-1	Archibald	39,790

FINAL LEAGUE POSITION: 8th in Division One

Appearances

Sub. Appearances

Goals

Clemence	Thomas	Mabbutt	Roberts	Stevens	Perryman	Hazard	Archibald	Galvin	Hoddle	Brazil	Falco	Bowen	Hughton	Crooks	Miler	O'Reilly	Brooke	Price	Crook	Dick	Cooke	Ardiles	Webster	Cockram	Parks	Culverhouse	Brace	
1	2	3	4	5	6	7*	8	9	10	11	12																	1
1	3	7	4	5	6		8	9	10	11*	12	2																2
1	3	7	4	5	6			9	10*		8		2	11	12													3
1		7	4	5	6			9			8		2	11		3	10											4
1		7	4	5	6			9			8	12	2	11		3	10*											5
1		7	4		6			9		12	8		2	11*		3	10	5										6
1		7	4	5	6		12	3	10	9	8		2				11*											7
1		7	4	5	6		8	3	10	11*	9		2				12											8
1		7	4*	5	6		8	3	10		9		2				11	12										9
1		7	4	5	6		8	3	10		9		2			12	11*											10
1		7	4	5	6		8	3	10		9		2	12			11*											11
1	3	7*	4	5	6		8	11	10		9		2	12														12
1	3		4	5	6		8	11	10	12	9		2						7*									13
1	3		4	5	6		8		10		9		2						7	11								14
1	3		4	5	6		8		10		9		2						11	7								15
1	3		4	5	6		8		10		9		2		12				11	7*								16
1	3		4	5	6		8*		10	11	9				2	12				7								17
1	3		4	5	6			7*	10	8	9				2				11		12							18
1			4	5	6		8		10		9	12	2*						11	3	7							19
1	3		4	5	6		8	7*	10	9	12					2			11									20
1	10			5	6		8		9	3						2			11			7	4					21
1	7		4		6		8		10		9	2	3		5	12								11*				22
			4	2	6		8	11	10*		9	3		12	5					7					1			23
		7	4	2	6		8	11	10		9	3			5										1			24
	12	7	4	2	6		8	11			9	3			5*									10	1			25
			4	2	6		8	11	10		9	3			5						7				1			26
			4	2	6		8	11	10		9	3			5					12	7*				1			27
	2			5	6		11*	10	8	9		3			4						7				1	12		28
	2		4		6	12	8		10	9		3			5					11*	7				1			29
	2		4		6	10	8			9		3			5				12	11*	7				1			30
1	2		4	7	6	10	8			9		3	12		5					11*								31
1	2	11	4	10	6	12	8			9		3			5*					7								32
1	2		4	10	6	7	8	11		9		3			5													33
	2		4	10	6	7		11		8	9	3			5										1			34
	2		4	8*	6	7		11		10	9	3			5		12								1			35
	2	10	4	12	6	7	8	11*		9		3			5										1			36
	2	10	4	12	6	7*	8	11		9		3			5										1			37
	2	7	4	12	6		8	9				3		11	5		10*								1			38
	2	10	4		6	7	8	11		9		3			5										1			39
	2	10	4		6		8	11		9*		3	12		5					7					1			40
1									10			3		11	5	4	8*		6	7				9		2	12	41
	2	7	4	10	6		8	11		9		3			5										1			42
26	26	21	35	37	41	9	31	30	24	17	32	6	34	6	20	9	7	1	3	10	9	8	1	2	16	1		
	1		3		2	1				2	4	1		4	1	3	5	1		1		1				1	1	
		2	6	4	1	2	21	1	4	3	13		3	1							2	1						

1984-85

1	Aug	25	(a)	Everton	W	4-1	Falco, Allen 2, Chiedozie	35,630
2		27	(h)	Leicester C	D	2-2	Roberts 2 (1 pen)	30,046
3	Sep	1	(h)	Norwich C	W	3-1	Chiedozie, Falco, Galvin	24,947
4		4	(a)	Sunderland	L	0-1		18,895
5		8	(a)	Sheffield W	L	1-2	Falco	33,421
6		15	(h)	Queen's Park R	W	5-0	Falco 2, Allen 2, Hazard	31,655
7		22	(a)	Aston Villa	W	1-0	Chiedozie	22,409
8		29	(h)	Luton T	W	4-2	Roberts (pen), Perryman, Falco, Hazard	30,204
9	Oct	6	(a)	Southampton	L	0-1		21,825
10		12	(h)	Liverpool	W	1-0	Crooks	28,599
11		20	(a)	Manchester U	L	0-1		54,516
12		27	(h)	Stoke C	W	4-0	Roberts (pen), Chiedozie, Allen 2	23,477
13	Nov	3	(h)	West Brom A	L	2-3	Chiedozie, Hazard	24,494
14		10	(a)	Nottingham F	W	2-1	Hazard, Galvin	21,306
15		17	(a)	Ipswich T	W	3-0	Mabbutt, Allen, Hoddle	21,894
16		24	(h)	Chelsea	D	1-1	Falco	31,197
17	Dec	1	(a)	Coventry C	D	1-1	Falco	14,518
18		8	(h)	Newcastle U	W	3-2	Roberts (pen), Falco 2	29,695
19		15	(a)	Watford	W	2-1	Falco, Crooks	24,225
20		22	(a)	Norwich C	W	2-1	Galvin, Crooks	17,682
21		26	(h)	West Ham U	D	2-2	Mabbutt, Crooks	37,186
22		29	(h)	Sunderland	W	2-0	Hoddle, Crooks	26,930
23	Jan	1	(a)	Arsenal	W	2-1	Falco, Crooks	48,714
24		12	(a)	Queen's Park R	D	2-2	Falco, Crooks	27,404
25	Feb	2	(a)	Luton T	D	2-2	Roberts, Falco	17,511
26		23	(a)	West Brom A	W	1-0	Falco	15,418
27	Mar	2	(a)	Stoke C	W	1-0	Crooks	12,552
28		12	(h)	Manchester U	L	1-2	Falco	42,918
29		16	(a)	Liverpool	W	1-0	Crooks	43,852
30		23	(h)	Southampton	W	5-1	Ardiles, Falco, Hoddle, Crooks, Brooke	33,772
31		30	(h)	Aston Villa	L	0-2		27,971
32	Apr	3	(h)	Everton	L	1-2	Roberts	48,108
33		6	(a)	West Ham U	D	1-1	Ardiles	24,435
34		13	(a)	Leicester C	W	2-1	Falco, Hoddle	15,609
35		17	(h)	Arsenal	L	0-2		40,399
36		20	(h)	Ipswich T	L	2-3	Leworthy 2	20,348
37		27	(a)	Chelsea	D	1-1	Galvin	26,310
38	May	4	(a)	Coventry C	W	4-2	Falco 2, Hoddle, Hughton	16,711
39		6	(a)	Newcastle U	W	3-2	Leworthy, Hoddle, Crooks	29,702
40		11	(h)	Watford	L	1-5	Hoddle (pen)	23,167
41		14	(h)	Sheffield W	W	2-0	Falco, Hoddle (pen)	15,669
42		17	(h)	Nottingham F	W	1-0	Falco	20,075

FINAL LEAGUE POSITION: 3rd in Division One

Appearances

Sub. Appearances

Goals

Clemence	Stevens	Hughton	Roberts	Miller	Perryman	Chiedozie	Falco	Allen	Hazard	Galvin	Mabbutt	Thomas	Crooks	Hoddle	Ardiles	Dick	Brooke	Bowen	Crook	Leworthy	
1	2	3	4	5	6	7	8	9	10*	11	12										1
1	2	3	4	5	6	7	8	9	10*	11	12										2
1	2	3	4	5	6	7*	8	9	10	11	12										3
1	2	3	4	5	6	7	8	9	10*	11		12									4
1	2	3	4	5	6	7	8*	9	10	11	12										5
1	2	3	4	5	6	7	8*	9	10	11	12										6
1	2	3		5	6	7	8		10	9	4		11								7
1	2	3	4	5	6	7	8		10	9			11								8
1	2	3*	4	5	6	7	8		10	9	12		11								9
1	2	3	4	5	6	7*	8		10	9	12		11								10
1	2	3	4	5	6		8		10	9	7			11*	12						11
1	2	3	4	5*	6	7	8	9	12	11				10							12
1	2*	3	4	5	6	7	8	9	10	11				12							13
1	2	12	4	5	6	7*	8	9	10	11	3										14
1	2		4	5	6	7	8	9	11		3			10							15
1	2		4	5	6	7	8	9	11		3			10							16
1	2	3	4	5	6	7	8	9	11*	12				10							17
1	2	3	4	5	6	7	8		9*	12		11	10								18
1	2	3	4	5	6	7	8		9	10	12	11*									19
1	2	3	4	5	6	7	8		12	9	10	11*									20
1	2	3*	4	5	6	7	8		12	9	10	11									21
1	2	12	4	5	6	7	8		9*	3		11	10								22
1	2		4	5	6	7	8	12	9	3		11	10*								23
1	2		4	5	6	7*	8		9	3		11	10	12							24
1	2	3	4		6	7*	8		12	9	5	11	10								25
1	2	3	4		6	7	8		12		5*	11	10		9						26
1	2	3	4	5	6	7	8					11	10		9						27
1	2*	3	4	5	6		8		12	9		11	10			7					28
1		3	4	5	6	7*	8		12	9	2	11	10								29
1		3	4	5	6		8			9	2	11	10	7*			12				30
1				5	6		8			9	2	11	10	7*			12	3	4		31
1			4	5	6		8			9	2	11*	10	7			12	3			32
1			4	5	6	12	8			9*	2	11	10	7				3			33
1			4	5	6	12	8			9	2	11*	10	7				3			34
1			4	5	6		8	12		11*	2		10	7				3		9	35
1			4	5*	6	12	8			11	2		10	7				3		9	36
1			4	5	6	3*	8			11	2		10	7					12	9	37
1		3	4	5	6		8			11	2		10							9	38
1		3	4	5	6	7*	8			11	2		10						12	9	39
1		3	4	5*	6		8			11	12	2	10	7						9	40
1		3	4	5	6	7*	8			11	9	2	10						12		41
1		3	4	5	6		8			11	9	2	10						7		42
42	28	29	40	39	42	31	42	12	15	38	15	14	22	26	10	2	1	6	2	6	
	2					3		1	8		10	2		2	1		3		3		
		1	7		1	5	22	7	4	4	2		10	8	2		1		1	3	

1985-86

1	Aug	17	(h)	Watford	W	4-0	P. Allen, Falco, Waddle 2	29,884
2		21	(a)	Oxford U	D	1-1	Thomas	10,634
3		24	(a)	Ipswich T	L	0-1		17,758
4		26	(h)	Everton	L	0-1		29,750
5		31	(a)	Manchester C	L	1-2	Miller	27,789
6	Sep	4	(h)	Chelsea	W	4-1	Roberts, Miller, Falco, Chiedozie	23,642
7		7	(h)	Newcastle U	W	5-1	Falco, Chiedozie 2, Hoddle, Hazard	23,883
8		14	(a)	Nottingham F	W	1-0	Hughton	17,554
9		21	(h)	Sheffield W	W	5-1	Falco 2, Hoddle (pen), Chiedozie	23,601
10		28	(a)	Liverpool	L	1-4	Chiedozie	41,521
11	Oct	5	(a)	West Brom A	D	1-1	Waddle	12,040
12		20	(a)	Coventry C	W	3-2	Falco, Hoddle (pen), Chiedozie	13,545
13		26	(h)	Leicester C	L	1-3	Falco	17,944
14	Nov	2	(a)	Southampton	L	0-1		17,440
15		9	(h)	Luton T	L	1-3	Cooke	19,163
16		16	(a)	Manchester U	D	0-0		54,575
17		23	(h)	Queen's Park R	D	1-1	Mabbutt	20,334
18		30	(a)	Aston Villa	W	2-1	Mabbutt, Falco	14,099
19	Dec	7	(h)	Oxford U	W	5-1	Falco, C. Allen 2, Hoddle, Waddle	17,698
20		14	(a)	Watford	L	0-1		16,327
21		21	(h)	Ipswich T	W	2-0	C. Allen, Hoddle	18,845
22		26	(h)	West Ham U	W	1-0	Perryman	33,835
23		28	(a)	Chelsea	L	0-2		37,115
24	Jan	1	(a)	Arsenal	D	0-0		45,109
25		11	(h)	Nottingham F	L	0-3		19,043
26		18	(h)	Manchester C	L	0-2		17,009
27	Feb	1	(a)	Everton	L	0-1		33,178
28		8	(h)	Coventry C	L	0-1		13,135
29		22	(a)	Sheffield W	W	2-1	Chiedozie, Howells	23,232
30	Mar	2	(h)	Liverpool	L	1-2	Waddle	16,436
31		8	(h)	West Brom A	W	5-0	Mabbutt, Falco 2, Galvin, Waddle	10,841
32		15	(a)	Birmingham C	W	2-1	Stevens, Waddle	9,394
33		22	(a)	Newcastle U	D	2-2	Hoddle, Waddle	30,645
34		29	(h)	Arsenal	W	1-0	Stevens	33,427
35		31	(a)	West Ham U	L	1-2	Ardiles	27,497
36	Apr	5	(a)	Leicester C	W	4-1	Bowen, Falco 3	9,574
37		12	(a)	Luton T	D	1-1	C. Allen	13,141
38		16	(h)	Birmingham C	W	2-0	Chiedozie, Falco	9,359
39		19	(h)	Manchester U	D	0-0		32,357
40		26	(a)	Queen's Park R	W	5-2	Falco 2, C. Allen 2, Hoddle	17,768
41	May	3	(h)	Aston Villa	W	4-2	Falco 2, C. Allen 2	14,854
42		5	(h)	Southampton	W	5-3	Galvin 3, C. Allen, Waddle	13,036

FINAL LEAGUE POSITION: 10th in Division One

Appearances

Sub. Appearances

Goals

Clemence	Thomas	Hughton	Allen P	Miller	Perryman	Ardiles	Falco	Waddle	Hazard	Galvin	Leworthy	Roberts	Hoddle	Crook	Chiedozie	Mabbutt	Stevens	Cooke	Allen C	Dick	Howells	Bowen	
1	2	3	4	5	6*	7	8	9	10	11	12												1
1	2	3	4	5	6	7	8	9	10	11													2
1	2	3	6	5		7	8	9	10	11*	12	4											3
1	2	3	6	5		7*	8	9		11		4	10		12								4
1	2	3	6	5		7	8	9		11*		4	10		12								5
1	2	3	6	5		7	8	11			12	4	10*		9								6
1	2	3	6	5		7	8*	11	12			4	10		9								7
1	2	3	6*	5	12	7	8	11				4	10		9								8
1	2	3	6	5		7*	8	11				4	10		9	12							9
1	2	3	5		6	7*	8	11				4	10		9	12							10
1	2	3	9	5	6	7	8*	11				4	10			12							11
1		3		5	6	7*	8	11		9		4	10		12		2						12
1		3		5	6		8	11		9		4	10		7		2						13
1		3			6	7	8	11		9*	10	4			12	5	2						14
1		3			6		8	11		9		4	10	7*		5	2		12				15
1		3	7		6		8	11		9		4	10			5	2						16
1		3	7		6		8	11		9		4	10			5	2						17
1		3	7		6		8	11				4	10			5	2		9				18
1	6	3	12			7	8	11				4*	10			5	2		9				19
1	2	3	7		6	12	8	11				4				5	10		9*				20
1	2	3	12		6	7	8	11					10*			5	4		9				21
1	2	3	12		6	7*	8	11					10			5	4		9				22
1	2*	3	7		6	12	8	11					10			5	4		9				23
1		3			6	7	8	11				4	10			5	2		9				24
1		3	8		6	7	11*					4	10		9	5	2		12				25
1		3	7	5	6		8	11				4	10		12		2		9*				26
1		3	12	5	6		8	11					10		7	4	2		9*				27
1			8	5	6			11				3*	10		7	4	2	12	9				28
1		3	2	5	6		8	11					10		7	4			9				29
1		3	2	5	6		8	11					10		7	4			9				30
1		3	2	5			8	11		9*		4	10		7		6		12				31
1		3	2	5			8	11		9		4	10		7		6						32
1		3	2*	5	12		8	11		9		4	10		7		6						33
1		3	2	5			8	11		9		4	10		7		6						34
1		3	2	5		10*	8	11		9		4			7		6		12				35
1		3	2	5		7*	8	11		9					12	4			10		6		36
1		3	2	5			8	11		9					7	4	6		10				37
1		3	2	5			8*	11					10		7	4	6		9			12	38
1	2	3		5			8	11				4	10		12	7	6		9*				39
1		3		5			8	11*		6		4	10		12	7	2		9				40
1	2	3		5			8	11		6		4	10		7				9				41
1	2	3		5			8	11		6		4	10*		7		12		9				42
42	27	33	29	29	22	20	40	39	3	23	2	32	31	1	13	29	28		16	1	1	1	
			4	1	3				1		3				3	5	3	1	2	3		1	
	1	1	1	2	1	1	19	11	1	4		1	7		7	3	2	1	9		1	1	

1986-87

#				Opponent		Res	Scorers	Att
1	Aug	23	(a)	Aston Villa	W	3-0	C. Allen 3	24,712
2		25	(h)	Newcastle U	D	1-1	C. Allen	25,381
3		30	(h)	Manchester C	W	1-0	Roberts	23,164
4	Sep	2	(a)	Southampton	L	0-2		17,911
5		6	(a)	Arsenal	D	0-0		44,703
6		13	(h)	Chelsea	L	1-3	C. Allen (pen)	28,202
7		20	(a)	Leicester C	W	2-1	C. Allen 2	13,141
8		27	(h)	Everton	W	2-0	C. Allen 2	28,007
9	Oct	4	(h)	Luton T	D	0-0		22,738
10		11	(a)	Liverpool	W	1-0	C. Allen	43,139
11		18	(h)	Sheffield W	D	1-1	C. Allen	26,876
12		25	(a)	Queen's Park R	L	0-2		18,579
13	Nov	1	(h)	Wimbledon	L	1-2	M. Thomas	21,820
14		8	(a)	Norwich C	L	1-2	Claesen	22,019
15		15	(h)	Coventry C	W	1-0	C. Allen	20,255
16		22	(a)	Oxford U	W	4-2	C. Allen 2, Waddle 2	12,143
17		29	(h)	Nottingham F	L	2-3	C. Allen 2	30,042
18	Dec	7	(a)	Manchester U	D	3-3	Mabbutt, C. Allen, Moran (og)	35,267
19		13	(h)	Watford	W	2-1	Gough, Hoddle	23,137
20		20	(a)	Chelsea	W	2-0	C. Allen 2	21,576
21		26	(h)	West Ham U	W	4-0	Hodge, C. Allen 2, Waddle	39,019
22		27	(a)	Coventry C	L	3-4	C. Allen 2, Claesen	22,175
23	Jan	1	(a)	Charlton A	W	2-0	Claesen, Galvin	19,744
24		4	(h)	Arsenal	L	1-2	M. Thomas	37,723
25		24	(a)	Aston Villa	W	3-0	Hodge 2, Claesen	19,121
26	Feb	14	(h)	Southampton	W	2-0	Hodge, Gough	22,066
27		25	(h)	Leicester C	W	5-0	C. Allen 2 (1 pen), P. Allen, Claesen 2	16,038
28	Mar	7	(h)	Queen's Park R	W	1-0	C. Allen (pen)	21,071
29		22	(h)	Liverpool	W	1-0	Waddle	32,763
30		25	(a)	Newcastle U	D	1-1	Hoddle	30,836
31		28	(a)	Luton T	L	1-3	Waddle	13,447
32	Apr	4	(h)	Norwich C	W	3-0	C. Allen 3	22,400
33		7	(a)	Sheffield W	W	1-0	C. Allen	19,488
34		15	(a)	Manchester C	D	1-1	Claesen	21,460
35		18	(h)	Charlton A	W	1-0	C. Allen	26,926
36		20	(a)	West Ham U	L	1-2	C. Allen	23,972
37		22	(a)	Wimbledon	D	2-2	Claesen, Bowen	7,917
38		25	(h)	Oxford U	W	3-1	P. Allen, Waddle, Hoddle	20,064
39	May	2	(a)	Nottingham F	L	0-2		19,837
40		4	(h)	Manchester U	W	4-0	M. Thomas 2, C. Allen (pen), P. Allen	36,692
41		9	(a)	Watford	L	0-1		20,024
42		11	(a)	Everton	L	0-1		28,287

FINAL LEAGUE POSITION: 3rd in Division One

Appearances

Sub. Appearances

Goals

50

Clemence	Stevens	Thomas M	Roberts	Gough	Mabbutt	Allen C	Falco	Waddle	Hoddle	Galvin	Allen P	Chiedozie	Thomas D	Ardiles	Howells	Claesen	Hughton	Miller	Polston	Close	Parks	Hodge	O'Shea	Bowen	Ruddock	Samways	Stimson	Moran	Gray	Moncur	
1	2	3	4	5	6	7	8	9	10*	11	12																				1
1	2	3	4	5	6	7	8	9	10	11																					2
1	2	3	4	5	6	7		9	10	11		8																			3
1	2	3	4*	5	6	7	8	9	10	11			12																		4
1	2	3	4	5	6	7	8*	9	10	11				12																	5
1	2	3	4	5*	6	7	8	9	10	11	12																				6
1	2*	3	4	5	6	7		9	10		11		8	12																	7
1		3	4	5	6	7	12	9	10	11*	8		2																		8
1		3	4	5	6			9	10	11	8*		2	12	7																9
1	2	3	4	5	6	7		9	10	11*	12					8															10
1	2	3	4	5	6	7		9	10	11						8															11
1	2*	3	4	5	6	7		9	10	11				12		8															12
1	2*	3	4	5	6	7		9	10	11				12		8															13
1		3	4	6	10	7		9	12	11						8	2*	5													14
1		3		5	6	7		9	10	11				12		8	2*		4												15
1		3		5	6	7		9	10		2		12	11		8*			4												16
1		3	4		6	7		9	10		2		12	11*				5	8												17
1		3	4	5	6	7		9	10	8	2		12	11*																	18
1		3	4	5	6	7		9	10	11*	8		2	12																	19
		3		5	6	7		9	10	11	8		2	4							1										20
1	3*			5	6	7		9	10	11	8		2	12								4									21
1				5	6	7		9	10	11	8		2	3*		12						4									22
1				5	6	7		9	10	12	8		2			11		3				4*									23
1		3		5	6	7		9	10	11	8		2	4*		12															24
1		3		5	6	7		9	10	12	8		2			11*						4									25
1		3		5	6	7		9	10		8		2	11*		12						4									26
1	10	3		5	6	7		9			8		2			11						4									27
1	10	3		5	6	7		9		11	8		2*			12						4									28
1	2	3		5	6	7		9	10		8					11						4									29
1	2	3		5	6	7		9	10		8					11						4									30
1	2	3		5	6	7		9	10		8		12			11						4*									31
1		3		5	6	7		9	10	12	8*					11	2					4									32
1	2	3		5	6	7		9	10		8					11*						4	12								33
1	2*	3		5	6	7		9	10		8					11						4		12							34
1		3		5		7			10	12	8			9*		11	2					4			6						35
1		3		5		7		9	10	11*	8					12	2			6		4			6						36
1		3		5	12					11	8			4		9*	2						7	10	6						37
1		3		5	6	7*		9	10		8					11	12	2				4									38
1		3		5				9		7*	8					11	10	2				4						6	12		39
1		3		5	6	7		9*	10		8					11	12	2				4									40
1	2	3		5	6	7		9	10		8					11*						4									41
	4															9	2		5	12	1				6	11	3	7*	8	10	42
40	20	39	17	40	37	38	5	39	35	20	34	1	13	15	1	18	9	2	6	1	2	19	1	1	4	1	1	1	1	1	
					1	1		1	4	3			4	9		8			1				1	1		1					
		4	1	2	1	33		6	3	1	3					8						4		1							

51

1987-88

#	Month	Date		Opponent	Result	Score	Scorers	Attendance
1	Aug	15	(a)	Coventry C	L	1-2	Mabbutt	23,947
2		19	(h)	Newcastle U	W	3-1	C. Allen, Waddle, Hodge	26,261
3		22	(h)	Chelsea	W	1-0	Claesen	37,079
4		29	(a)	Watford	D	1-1	C. Allen (pen)	19,073
5	Sep	1	(h)	Oxford U	W	3-0	C. Allen, Claesen 2	21,811
6		5	(a)	Everton	D	0-0		32,389
7		12	(h)	Southampton	W	2-1	C. Allen (pen), Claesen	24,728
8		19	(a)	West Ham U	W	1-0	Fairclough	27,750
9		26	(a)	Manchester U	L	0-1		47,601
10	Oct	3	(h)	Sheffield W	W	2-0	P. Allen, Claesen	24,311
11		10	(a)	Norwich C	L	1-2	Claesen	18,669
12		18	(h)	Arsenal	L	1-2	Claesen	36,680
13		24	(a)	Nottingham F	L	0-3		23,543
14		31	(h)	Wimbledon	L	0-3		22,282
15	Nov	4	(a)	Portsmouth	D	0-0		15,302
16		14	(h)	Queen's Park R	D	1-1	P. Allen	28,113
17		21	(a)	Luton T	L	0-2		10,091
18		28	(h)	Liverpool	L	0-2		47,362
19	Dec	13	(h)	Charlton A	L	0-1		20,392
20		20	(a)	Derby Co	W	2-1	C. Allen, Claesen	17,593
21		26	(a)	Southampton	L	1-2	Fairclough	18,456
22		28	(h)	West Ham U	W	2-1	Fairclough, Waddle	39,456
23	Jan	1	(h)	Watford	W	2-1	C. Allen, Moran	25,235
24		2	(a)	Chelsea	D	0-0		29,317
25		16	(h)	Coventry C	D	2-2	C. Allen 2	25,650
26		23	(a)	Newcastle U	L	0-2		24,616
27	Feb	13	(a)	Oxford U	D	0-0		9,906
28		23	(h)	Manchester U	D	1-1	C. Allen	25,731
29		27	(a)	Sheffield W	W	3-0	C. Allen, P. Allen, Claesen	18,046
30	Mar	1	(h)	Derby Co	D	0-0		15,986
31		6	(a)	Arsenal	L	1-2	C. Allen	37,143
32		9	(h)	Everton	W	2-1	Fairclough, Walsh	18,662
33		12	(h)	Norwich C	L	1-3	Claesen	19,322
34		19	(a)	Wimbledon	L	0-3		8,616
35		26	(h)	Nottingham F	D	1-1	Foster (og)	25,306
36	Apr	2	(h)	Portsmouth	L	0-1		18,616
37		4	(a)	Queen's Park R	L	0-2		14,738
38		23	(a)	Liverpool	L	0-1		44,798
39	May	2	(a)	Charlton A	D	1-1	Hodge	13,977
40		4	(h)	Luton T	W	2-1	Mabbutt, Hodge	15,437

FINAL LEAGUE POSITION: 13th in Division One

Appearances

Sub. Appearances

Goals

Clemence	Stevens	Thomas	Gough	Fairclough	Mabbutt	Allen C	Allen P	Waddle	Hodge	Claesen	Metgod	Ardiles	Polston	Moran	Samways	Close	Howells	Parks	Hughton	Moncur	Ruddock	O'Shea	Statham	Fenwick	Mimms	Walsh	Gray	
1	2	3	4	5	6	7	8*	9	10	11†	12	13																1
1	2*	3	4	5	6	7	8	9	10		11	12																2
1		3	4	5	6	7	8	9	10	12	11*	2																3
1		3	4	5	6	7	8	9	10	11		2																4
1		3*	4	5	6	/	8!	9	10	11	13	2	12															5
1		3	4	5	6	7	8	9	10*	11	12	2																6
1	2*	3	4	5	6	7	8		10	11	12	9																7
1	2	3	4	5		7†	8		10	11	12	9		6*	13													8
1	2	3	4	5	6		8		10	11	13	9†		7*	12													9
1	2	3		5	6	7*	8		10	11		9		4	12													10
1	2	3		5	6		8		10	11		9*		4	7	12												11
	2	3		5	6	13	8	9	10†	11		4		12	7*			1										12
	10	3		5	6	7	8			11		9		4†	12			1	2*	13								13
	10	3*		5	6	7	8			11		9		4†	12			1	2			13						14
	2			5	6	12	8			11		9	7*	10				1	3		4							15
	2			5	6	7	8		10	11*		9		12				1	3		4							16
	2*	12		5	6	7	8†		10			9		4	13	11		1	3									17
	11	3		5	6	7	8	9	10	12								1	2*			4†	13					18
	10	3		5	6	7	8	9		11				4				1	2									19
	2	3		5	6*	7	8†	9		11		10		13	4			1	12									20
	6	3		5		7†		9	8			10		11	4*	13		1	2				12					21
	6*	3		5			8	9	4			10		7†		13	11	1	2				12					22
		3		5	6	7	8	9	4			10		11*		12		1					2					23
		3		5	6	7*	8†	9	10					11		12		1	2		13			4				24
		3		5	6	7	8	9				10*		11†		13		1	2		12			4				25
		3		5	6	7	8	9				10		11†		13		1	2*		12			4				26
		3		5	6	7	8	9		11					10			1					2	4				27
		3		5	6	7	8	9							10								2	4	1	11		28
		3		5	6	7	8		12						10					9			2	4	1	11*		29
		3		5	6	7	8								10					9*			2	4	1	11		30
		3		5	6	7	8							9	10								2	4	1	11		31
		3		5	6	7	8							9	10*					12			2	4	1	11		32
		3		5	6	7	8					12		9	10*								2	4	1	11		33
		3		5	6	7	8				12			9*	10								2	4	1	11		34
		3		5	6		8		9	11†					12	10	13						2	4*	1	7		35
				5	6		8		9†	11					13	10	12		3*				2	4	1	7		36
				5	6		8	13	9*			3			12	10	11†						2	4	1	7		37
		3		5	6	12	8	9	11			4*			10								2		1	7		38
		3		5	6	7*	8	9	11	12	13				10†								2	4	1			39
		3		5	6	7†	8	9	11			10			12								2	4*	1		13	40
11	18	35	9	40	37	31	39	21	25	19	5	26		9	21	2	3	16	12	3	3		14	17	13	11		
		1	3					1	1	5	7	2	2	4	5	5	8		1	2	2	1	4				1	
				4	2	11	3	2	3	10				1												1		

1988-89

1	Sep	3	(a)	Newcastle U	D	2-2	Fenwick, Waddle	32,977
2		10	(h)	Arsenal	L	2-3	Gascoigne, Waddle	32,621
3		17	(a)	Liverpool	D	1-1	Fenwick	40,929
4		24	(h)	Middlesbrough	W	3-2	Fenwick (pen), Waddle, Howells	23,427
5	Oct	1	(h)	Manchester U	D	2-2	Walsh, Waddle	29,318
6		8	(a)	Charlton A	D	2-2	Fenwick (pen), Allen	14,384
7		22	(a)	Norwich C	L	1-3	Fairclough	20,330
8		25	(h)	Southampton	L	1-2	Ray Wallace (og)	19,517
9		29	(a)	Aston Villa	L	1-2	Fenwick	26,238
10	Nov	5	(h)	Derby Co	L	1-3	Stewart	22,868
11		12	(h)	Wimbledon	W	3-2	Butters, Fenwick (pen), Samways	23,589
12		20	(a)	Sheffield W	W	2-0	Stewart 2	15,386
13		23	(h)	Coventry C	D	1-1	Stewart	21,961
14		26	(h)	Queen's Park R	D	2-2	Gascoigne, Waddle	26,698
15	Dec	3	(a)	Everton	L	0-1		29,657
16		10	(h)	Millwall	W	2-0	Gascoigne, Waddle	27,660
17		17	(a)	West Ham U	W	2-0	Thomas, Mabbutt	28,365
18		26	(h)	Luton T	D	0-0		27,337
19		31	(h)	Newcastle U	W	2-0	Walsh, Waddle	27,739
20	Jan	2	(a)	Arsenal	L	0-2		45,129
21		15	(h)	Nottingham F	L	1-2	Waddle	16,903
22		21	(a)	Middlesbrough	D	2-2	Stewart 2	23,692
23	Feb	5	(a)	Manchester U	L	0-1		41,423
24		11	(h)	Charlton A	D	1-1	Stewart	22,803
25		21	(h)	Norwich C	W	2-1	Gascoigne, Waddle	19,126
26		25	(a)	Southampton	W	2-0	Nayim, Waddle	16,702
27	Mar	1	(h)	Aston Villa	W	2-1	Waddle 2	19,090
28		11	(a)	Derby Co	D	1-1	Gascoigne	18,206
29		18	(a)	Coventry C	D	1-1	Waddle	17,156
30		22	(a)	Nottingham F	W	2-1	Howells, Samways	23,098
31		26	(h)	Liverpool	L	1-2	Fenwick (pen)	30,012
32		28	(a)	Luton T	W	3-1	Howells, Walsh, Gascoigne	11,146
33	Apr	1	(h)	West Ham U	W	3-0	Fenwick (pen), Nayim, Stewart	28,375
34		12	(h)	Sheffield W	D	0-0		17,270
35		15	(a)	Wimbledon	W	2-1	Waddle, Stewart	12,366
36		22	(h)	Everton	W	2-1	Walsh 2	28,568
37		29	(a)	Millwall	W	5-0	Walsh, Stewart 3, Samways	16,551
38	May	13	(a)	Queen's Park R	L	0-1		21,873

FINAL LEAGUE POSITION: 6th in Division One

Appearances

Sub. Appearances

Goals

Mimms	Statham	Hughton	Fenwick	Fairclough	Mabbutt	Walsh	Gascoigne	Waddle	Thomas	Allen	Moran	Howells	Samways	Stewart	Stevens	Moncur	Stimson	Butters	Gray	Robson	Polston J	Bergsson	Thorstvedt	Nayim	No.
1	2	3	4	5	6	7*	8†	9	10	11	12	13													1
1	2*		4	5	6	7	8	9	3	11	13	12	10†												2
1	2	12	4	5	6	7*	8	9†	3	11		13	10												3
1	2		4	5	6	7†	8	9	3	11	13	12	10												4
1	2	5	4		6	7	8*	9†	3	11		12	10	13											5
1	2		4		6	7*	8	9	3	5		12	10	11											6
1			4	5	6		8	9	3	11		12	10*	7	2										7
1			4	5	6	7	8	9	3	11				10	2										8
1			4	5	6		8	9	3	11†		7*		10	2	12	13								9
1			4	5	6		8	9	3	11†	7*	12	13	10	2										10
1			4	5	6		8	9	3		7		11	10	2*			12							11
1			4	5	6		8†	9	3	13	7*	12	11	10				2							12
1			4	5	6	12	8	9	3	13	7*	11†		10				2							13
1			4	5	6	7†	8	9	3*	11		12		10				2	13						14
1			4	5	6	12	8	9	3	11	7*			10				2							15
1			4	5	6	7	8	9	3	11				10				2							16
1			4	5	6	7*	8†	9	3	11				10				2		12	13				17
1			4		6	7*	8†	9	3	11	12	13		10				2				5			18
1			4	5	6	7*		9	3	11	12			10				2				8			19
1			4	5	6	7		9	3	11				10				2				8			20
		3*	4	5	6	7†	12	9		11	13			10				2				8	1		21
		3	4		6	12	8†	9	13	11	7*			10				2				5	1		22
		3	4		6	13	8	9	12	11	7†			10				2				5*	1		23
		3	4		6	12	8	9		11	7*			10				2				5	1		24
		3			6	7	8	9	5	11	12							2		10*			1	4	25
		3		5	6	7		9	8	11	12							2		10*			1	4	26
		3	4	5	6	7		9		11								2		10			1	8	27
		3	4		6	7†	8	9	12	11				10				2		13			1	5*	28
		3	4		6	7	8*	9		11	12			10				2					1	5	29
		3	4		6	7		9		11	8	12		10				2					1	5*	30
		3	4		6	7†		9		11	8	13		10				2			12		1	5*	31
		3	4		6	7	8	9		11	5			10				2					1		32
		3	4		6	7	8	9		11	12			10				2					1	5*	33
		3			6	7	8	9		11	5	10						2				4	1		34
		3	4		6	7	8	9		11	5			10				2					1		35
		3	4		6	7	8*	9		11†	5	12		10				2					1	13	36
		3	4*		6	7	8	9†		11	5	12		10				2					1	13	37
		3			6	7	8*	9		11†	5	4		10				2			13		1	12	38
20	6	20	34	20	38	28	31	38	22	35	4	12	12	29	5			27		3		8	18	8	
	1				5	1		3	2	4	15	7	1		1	1	1	1	1	2	3			3	
			8	1	1	6	6	14	1	1		3	3	12				1						2	

1989-90

#	Month	Date		Opponent		Result	Scorers	Attendance
1	Aug	19	(h)	Luton T	W	2-1	Stewart, Allen	17,665
2		22	(a)	Everton	L	1-2	Allen	34,402
3		26	(a)	Manchester C	D	1-1	Gascoigne	32,004
4	Sep	9	(a)	Aston Villa	L	0-2		24,769
5		16	(h)	Chelsea	L	1-4	Gascoigne	16,260
6		23	(a)	Norwich C	D	2-2	Gascoigne, Lineker	20,095
7		30	(h)	Queen's Park R	W	3-2	Lineker 3	23,781
8	Oct	14	(a)	Charlton A	W	3-1	Gascoigne, Lineker, Thomas	17,692
9		18	(h)	Arsenal	W	2-1	Walsh, Samways	33,944
10		21	(h)	Sheffield W	W	3-0	Lineker 2, Moran	26,909
11		29	(a)	Liverpool	L	0-1		26,550
12	Nov	4	(a)	Southampton	D	1-1	Gascoigne	19,601
13		11	(h)	Wimbledon	L	0-1		26,876
14		18	(a)	Crystal Palace	W	3-2	Howells, Samways, Lineker (pen)	26,366
15		25	(h)	Derby Co	L	1-2	Stewart	28,075
16	Dec	2	(a)	Luton T	D	0-0		12,620
17		9	(h)	Everton	W	2-1	Stewart, Lineker	29,374
18		16	(a)	Manchester U	W	1-0	Linker	36,230
19		26	(h)	Millwall	W	3-1	Samways, Lineker, McLeary (og)	26,874
20		30	(h)	Nottingham F	L	2-3	Lineker 2	33,401
21	Jan	1	(a)	Coventry C	D	0-0		19,599
22		13	(h)	Manchester C	D	1-1	Howells	26,384
23		20	(a)	Arsenal	L	0-1		46,132
24	Feb	4	(h)	Norwich C	W	4-0	Lineker 3 (1 pen), Howells	19,599
25		10	(a)	Chelsea	W	2-1	Howells, Lineker	29,130
26		21	(h)	Aston Villa	L	0-2		32,472
27		24	(a)	Derby Co	L	1-2	Moncur	19,676
28	Mar	3	(h)	Crystal Palace	L	0-1		26,181
29		10	(h)	Charlton A	W	3-0	J. Polston, Lineker, Howells	21,104
30		17	(a)	Queen's Park R	L	1-3	Walsh	16,691
31		21	(h)	Liverpool	W	1-0	Stewart	25,656
32		31	(a)	Sheffield W	W	4-2	Allen, Lineker 2, Stewart	26,582
33	Apr	7	(a)	Nottingham F	W	3-1	Stewart, Allen 2	21,669
34		14	(h)	Coventry C	W	3-2	Lineker 2, Stewart	23,317
35		16	(a)	Millwall	W	1-0	Lineker	10,573
36		21	(h)	Manchester U	W	2-1	Gascoigne, Lineker	33,317
37		28	(a)	Wimbledon	L	0-1		12,800
38	May	5	(h)	Southampton	W	2-1	Stewart, Allen	31,038

FINAL LEAGUE POSITION: 3rd in Division One

Appearances

Sub. Appearances

Goals

Thorsvedt	Butters	Bergsson	Fenwick	Howells	Mabbutt	Samways	Gascoigne	Stewart	Lineker	Allen	Walsh	Sedgley	Stevens	Van den Hauwe	Thomas	Robson	Nayim	Moran	Polston J	Mimms	Hughton	Moncur	Polston A	
1	2	3	4	5	6	7*	8†	9	10	11	12	13												1
1	2		4	5	6	12	8†	9	10	11	13	7*	3											2
1	2		4	5*	6	13	8	9	10	11†	12	7	3											3
1	2*		4	5	6	7*	8	9	10	11	13		12	3										4
1			4	5†	6		8	9	10	11	7			3*	2	12	13							5
1	2		4		6	7*	8	9	10†		13	11		3	5	12								6
1	2		4		6		8	9	10	12		11		3	5*		7							7
1	2*		4		6	13	8	9	10	5		11		3	12		7†							8
1			4	12	6	9*	8		10	5	7	11		3	2									9
1			4	7	6	9	8*		10	5		11		3	2		12							10
1		4		7	6	9			10	5*	13	11		3	2		8†	12						11
1		4		7	6	9*	8		10	5	12	11		3	2									12
1		4		5	6	9†	8	12	10	13	7*	11		3	2									13
1		4		5	6	7	8	9	10*		12			3	2				11					14
1				5*	6	7†	8	9	10	11	12	4		3	2				13					15
1		3		5	6	7	8	9	10*	4	12	11			2									16
1		12		5	6	7*	8	9	10	4		11		3	2									17
				5	6	7	8	9	10	4		11		3	2					1				18
		3		5	6	7	8	9	10	4		11	12		2*					1				19
		2*		5	6	7†	8	9	10	4	13	11	12	3						1				20
		2		5	6	7	8*	9	10	4		11		3			12			1				21
1				5		7		9	10	4		11		3	2		8				6			22
1				5	6	7†		9	10	4	12	11		3*	2		13	8						23
1				5	6		8		10*		7	11		3			9	12	4		2			24
1				5	6		8		10†		7*	11		3			9	12	4		2	13		25
1				5	6		8*		10		7	11		3			9†	13	4		2	12		26
1				5	6				10	12	7	11†		3	13		9		4		2*	8		27
1				5	6		8*		10		7			3		12	9		4		2	11†	13	28
1				5	6		8		10	11	7			3			9		4		2			29
1				5	6		8	12	10	11	7			3			9		4†		2*	13		30
1		2		5*	6		8	13	10	11	7†	4		3	12		9							31
1		2		5	6		8	12	10	11	7*	4		3	13		9†							32
1		2		5*	6		8	7†	10	11	13	4		3	12		9							33
1		2			6		8	7	10	11		4		3	5		9							34
1		2		5	6		8*	7	10	11	13	4		3	12		9†							35
1		2		5	6	12	8	7	10	11		4		3			9*							36
1		2*		5		12	8	7	10	11		4		3†	13		9		6					37
1		2*		5	6		8	7	10	11		4		3	12		9							38
34	7	17	10	33	36	18	34	24	38	29	12	31	4	31	17		18		11	4	8	2		
	1		1		5		4			3	14	1	3		9	3	1	5	2			3	1	
				5		3	6	8	24	6	2				1			1	1			1		

57

1990-91

#	Month	Date		Opponent	Result		Scorers	Attendance
1	Aug	25	(h)	Manchester C	W	3-1	Gascoigne, Lineker 2	33,501
2		28	(a)	Sunderland	D	0-0		30,214
3	Sep	1	(a)	Arsenal	D	0-0		40,009
4		8	(h)	Derby Co	W	3-0	Gascoigne 3	23,614
5		15	(a)	Leeds U	W	2-0	Howells, Lineker	31,342
6		22	(h)	Crystal Palace	D	1-1	Gascoigne	34,859
7		29	(h)	Aston Villa	W	2-1	Lineker, Allen	34,939
8	Oct	6	(a)	Queen's Park R	D	0-0		21,405
9		20	(h)	Sheffield U	W	4-0	Nayim, Walsh 3	34,612
10		27	(a)	Nottingham F	W	2-1	Howells 2	27,347
11	Nov	4	(h)	Liverpool	L	1-3	Lineker	35,003
12		10	(h)	Wimbledon	W	4-2	Mabbutt, Stewart, Lineker (pen), Walsh	28,769
13		18	(a)	Everton	D	1-1	Howells	23,716
14		24	(h)	Norwich C	W	2-1	Lineker 2	33,942
15	Dec	1	(a)	Chelsea	L	2-3	Gascoigne, Lineker	33,478
16		8	(h)	Sunderland	D	3-3	Lineker, Walsh 2	30,431
17		15	(a)	Manchester C	L	1-2	Gascoigne	31,236
18		22	(h)	Luton T	W	2-1	Stewart 2	27,007
19		26	(a)	Coventry C	L	0-2		22,731
20		29	(a)	Southampton	L	0-3		21,405
21	Jan	1	(h)	Manchester U	L	1-2	Lineker (pen)	29,399
22		12	(h)	Arsenal	D	0-0		34,753
23		20	(a)	Derby Co	W	1-0	Lineker	17,747
24	Feb	2	(h)	Leeds U	D	0-0		32,253
25		23	(a)	Wimbledon	L	1-5	Bergsson	10,500
26	Mar	2	(h)	Chelsea	D	1-1	Lineker (pen)	26,168
27		16	(a)	Aston Villa	L	2-3	Samways, Allen	32,638
28		23	(h)	Queen's Park R	D	0-0		30,860
29		30	(h)	Coventry C	D	2-2	Nayim 2	29,033
30	Apr	1	(a)	Luton T	D	0-0		11,322
31		6	(h)	Southampton	W	2-0	Lineker 2	24,291
32		10	(a)	Norwich C	L	1-2	Hendry	19,014
33		17	(a)	Crystal Palace	L	0-1		26,285
34		20	(a)	Sheffield U	D	2-2	Edinburgh, Walsh	25,706
35		24	(h)	Everton	D	3-3	Allen, Mabbutt, Nayim	21,675
36	May	4	(h)	Nottingham F	D	1-1	Nayim	30,891
37		11	(a)	Liverpool	L	0-2		36,192
38		20	(a)	Manchester U	D	1-1	Hendry	46,791

FINAL LEAGUE POSITION: 11th in Division One

Appearances

Sub. Appearances

Goals

Thorstvedt	Bergsson	Van den Hauwe	Sedgley	Howells	Mabbutt	Stewart	Gacoigne	Nayim	Lineker	Allen	Samways	Walsh	Thomas	Moncur	Edinburgh	Tuttle	Moran	Fenwick	Gray	Hendon	Walker	Hendry	Garland	Match
1	2	3	4	5	6	7	8	9	10	11*	12													1
1	2	3	4	5	6	7*	8	9†	10	11	13	12												2
1	2	3	4	5	6	7	8*	9	10	11			12											3
1	?	3	4	5	6	7*	8	9†	10	11	13	12												4
1	2	3	4	5	6	7	8	9	10	11														5
1	2	3	4	5	6	7	8	9	10	11														6
1	2*	3	4	5†	6	7	8	9	10	11	12	13												7
1		3	4	5	6	7*	8	9†	10	11	12	2	13											8
1		3	4	5	6	7	8*	9		11	10	2	12											9
1		3	4*	5	6	7	8	9	10	11	12	2												10
1	2*	3	4	5	6	7	8	9†	10	11	13	12												11
1		3*	4†	5	6	7	8	9	10	11		13	2		12									12
1		3	4	5	6	7	8	9	10*	11		12	2											13
1		3	4	5	6	7	8	9	10	11			2											14
1		3		5	6	7	8	9†	10	11		13	2		12	4*								15
1		3		5	6	7†	8	9	10	11	13	12	2		4*									16
1		3	4	5*	6	7	8	9†	10	13	12	11	2											17
1		3	4	5	6	7	8	9	10*	13	12	11†	2											18
1		3	4*	5	6	7	8	12	10	9	13	11†	2											19
1	12	3	4	5*	6	7		9†	10	11	8	13	2											20
1		3	4*	5	6	7	8	9	10	11			2				12							21
1				5	6	7	8		10	11		9	2	3				4						22
1	13	4	5		7		6*	10†	11	8	9	12			3			2						23
1		3	4		6	7		5*	10	11	12	9	8					2						24
1	2		4		6			5*	10	11	7		8	9	3				12					25
1		3	4		6	7	8*	5	10	11		13	12	2					9†					26
1		3	4		6	7		10†	11	8		5	9	2*					13	12				27
1			4		6	7		5*	10	11	8	13	3	12	2				9†					28
1		3	4*		6	7		5		11	8	10	13	12	2				9†					29
1		3			6	7		5		11	8	10	2	9	4									30
1		3	4		6	7			10	11	8†	9	5*	13	2				12					31
	3*	4	2			8†	7				9	5	11		6					12	1	10	13	32
1		3*	4		6	7	8†	5		11		9	10	2		12						13		33
1	12		4	5		7		8		11	9*	10	3		2	6						13		34
1		13	5	6	7		4	10†	11	9	8*	3		2	12							13		35
1		3*	4	5	6			8	7	10	11	9	12		2									36
1		3	4	5*	6	7	8		10†	11	9	12			2							13		37
1	12		4	5	6*	7			10†		9	8	13		2			3				11		38
37	9	31	33	29	35	35	26	32	32	34	14	16	23	4	14	4		4	3		1	2		
	3	1	1				1		2	9	13	8	5	2	2	1		3	2		2	1		
	1			4	2	3	7	5	15	3	1	7		1				2						

59

1991-92

#	Month	Date		Opponent	Res	Score	Scorers	Att
1	Aug	17	(a)	Southampton	W	3-2	Durie, Lineker 2	18,581
2		24	(h)	Chelsea	L	1-3	Lineker	34,645
3		28	(a)	Nottingham F	W	3-1	Durie, Lineker, Bergsson	24,018
4		31	(a)	Norwich C	W	1-0	Lineker	19,460
5	Sep	7	(a)	Aston Villa	D	0-0		33,096
6		14	(h)	Queen's Park R	W	2-0	Lineker 2	30,059
7		21	(a)	Wimbledon	W	5-3	Samways, Lineker 4 (1 pen)	11,927
8		28	(h)	Manchester U	L	1-2	Durie	35,087
9	Oct	5	(a)	Everton	L	1-3	Lineker	29,505
10		19	(h)	Manchester C	L	0-1		30,502
11		26	(a)	West Ham U	L	1-2	Lineker	23,946
12	Nov	2	(a)	Sheffield W	D	0-0		31,573
13		16	(h)	Luton T	W	4-1	Lineker 2, Houghton 2	27,543
14		23	(h)	Sheffield U	L	0-1		28,168
15	Dec	1	(a)	Arsenal	L	0-2		38,892
16		7	(h)	Notts Co	W	2-1	Mabbutt, Walsh	23,364
17		14	(a)	Leeds U	D	1-1	Howells	31,404
18		18	(h)	Liverpool	L	1-2	Walsh	27,434
19		22	(a)	Crystal Palace	W	2-1	Walsh, Lineker	22,491
20		26	(h)	Nottingham F	L	1-2	Stewart	31,079
21		28	(h)	Norwich C	W	3-0	Nayim, Lineker, Allen	27,969
22	Jan	1	(a)	Coventry C	W	2-1	Stewart, Lineker	19,639
23		11	(a)	Chelsea	L	0-2		28,628
24		18	(h)	Southampton	L	1-2	Mabbutt	23,191
25		25	(h)	Oldham A	D	0-0		20,843
26	Feb	1	(a)	Manchester C	L	0-1		30,123
27		16	(h)	Crystal Palace	L	0-1		19,834
28		22	(h)	Arsenal	D	1-1	Stewart	33,124
29	Mar	7	(h)	Leeds U	L	1-3	Allen	27,622
30		11	(a)	Luton T	D	0-0		11,494
31		14	(h)	Sheffield W	L	0-2		23,047
32		21	(a)	Liverpool	L	1-2	Stewart	39,968
33		28	(h)	Coventry C	W	4-3	Durie 3, Lineker	22,744
34	Apr	1	(h)	West Ham U	W	3-0	Lineker 3	31,809
35		4	(h)	Aston Villa	L	2-5	Lineker, Teale (og)	26,370
36		7	(a)	Notts Co	W	2-0	Lineker 2	9,205
37		11	(a)	Queen's Park R	W	2-1	A. Gray, Durie	20,678
38		14	(a)	Sheffield U	L	0-2		21,526
39		18	(h)	Wimbledon	W	3-2	Lineker 2, Hendry	23,934
40		20	(a)	Oldham A	L	0-1		15,443
41		25	(h)	Everton	D	3-3	Stewart, Minton, Allen	36,340
42	May	2	(a)	Manchester U	L	1-3	Lineker	44,595

FINAL LEAGUE POSITION: 15th in Division One

Appearances

Sub. Appearances

Goals

Thorstvedt	Fenwick	Van den Hauwe	Sedgley	Howells	Mabbutt	Stewart	Durie	Samways	Lineker	Allen	Nayim	Bergsson	Walker	Hendry	Hendon	Tuttle	Houghton	Edinburgh	Walsh	Gray A	Cundy	Minton	No.
1	2	3	4	5*	6	7	8	9	10	11†	12	13											1
1	2*	3		5	6	7	8	9	10	11	4	12											2
	2	3		5	6	7	8*	9	10	11†	4	13	1	12									3
	2	3		5	6	7	8	9	10		4	11	1										4
	2	3		5	6	7	8	9	10		4	11	1										5
	2	3	13	5*	6	7	8	9†	10	12	4	11	1										6
		3	5		6	7	8	9	10	11†	4	2	1	12									7
		3	12		6	7	8	9	10	11	4*	2†	1			5		13					8
1		3	12		6	7	8	9†	10	11	4*	2				13		5					9
1	3†	7	13	6		8	9	10	11	4*	5							2	12				10
1	3†	5		6	7	8	9	10	11	4*	13							2	12				11
1	3	4†	5	6	7	8		10*	11	9	13							2	12				12
1	3	4	5*	6			9	10	11†	12	7	13						2	8				13
1	3	12	5*	6		8	9	10		4†	7	13						2	11				14
1	2	3		5	6	7	8	9*	11	12	4							10					15
1	2	3	13	5*	6	7	8	9†	11	12	4							10					16
1	2	3	13	5	6	7	8†	9*	11	12	4							10					17
1	2	3		5*	6	7		9	10	11	12	4							8				18
1	2	13	5	6	7			9	10*	11	12	4						3†	8				19
1	2	3	13	5	6	7		9*	10	11	12	4†							8				20
1	2	3	4		6	7		9	10	11	5							12	8*				21
1	2	3	4	5	6	7		9†	10	11							12	13	8*				22
1	2	3	4	5†	6	7*		9	11	10	12							13	8				23
	3*		4		6	7	8	9†	10	11	12		1				13	2	5				24
	3		4		6	7	8		10	11	5*		1				12	2	9				25
	3		4	5*		7	8	9†	10	11	13	6	1					2	12				26
1	2	3	4	5†	6	7	8	9*	10	11	13							12					27
1	2	3	4	5	6	7	8		10	11	9*							12					28
1	2	3†	4	5	6	7	8		10*	11		13							12	9			29
1	2		4	5	6	7	8			11		12						3	10*	9			30
1	2†		4		6	7	8			11	9*	13					12	3	10	5			31
1	2	10	4	5*	6	7	8			11								3	12	9			32
1	2	13			6	7	8	10†	11	9								3	12	4*	5		33
	2†	13			6	7	8	10	11	9			1					3	12	4*	5		34
				7	6		8*	10	11	9		2	1					3	12	4	5		35
	2	12		9	6	7		10†	11				1	13				3	8*	4	5		36
	2	13	9*	6†	7	8		10	11				1		12			3	12	4	5		37
	13	2	6	9*		7	8†	10	11				1		12			3		4	5		38
	2	13			6	7		10	11	9			1		12			3	8*	4†	5		39
	2†	12			6	7	13	10	11	9			1		8*			3		4	5		40
	2	12			6	7	8	10	11				1					3	13	4†	5	9*	41
	2	12			6	7	8	10	11				1					3		4	5	9*	42
24	22	35	21	27	40	38	31	26	35	38	22	17	18	1		2		22	17	14	10	2	
1		13	4				1		1	9	11		4	2			10	1	12				
			1	2	5	7	1		28	3	1	1					1		2	3	1	1	

1992-93

1	Aug	15	(a)	Southampton	D	0-0		16,654
2		19	(h)	Coventry C	L	0-2		24,388
3		22	(h)	Crystal Palace	D	2-2	Durie, Sedgley	25,237
4		25	(a)	Leeds U	L	0-5		28,218
5		30	(a)	Ipswich T	D	1-1	Cundy	20,100
6	Sep	2	(h)	Sheffield U	W	2-0	Sheringham, Durie	21,322
7		5	(h)	Everton	W	2-1	Allen, Turner	26,503
8		14	(a)	Coventry C	L	0-1		15,348
9		19	(h)	Manchester U	D	1-1	Durie	33,296
10		27	(a)	Sheffield W	L	0-2		24,895
11	Oct	3	(a)	Queen's Park R	L	1-4	Sheringham	19,845
12		17	(h)	Middlesbrough	D	2-2	Sheringham (pen), Barmby	24,735
13		25	(a)	Wimbledon	D	1-1	Barmby	8,628
14		31	(h)	Liverpool	W	2-0	Nayim, Ruddock	32,917
15	Nov	7	(a)	Blackburn R	W	2-0	Howells, Sheringham (pen)	17,305
16		21	(h)	Aston Villa	D	0-0		32,852
17		28	(a)	Manchester C	W	1-0	Watson	25,496
18	Dec	5	(h)	Chelsea	L	1-2	Campbell	31,540
19		12	(h)	Arsenal	W	1-0	Allen	33,707
20		19	(a)	Oldham A	L	1-2	Sheringham	11,735
21		26	(a)	Norwich C	D	0-0		19,413
22		28	(h)	Nottingham F	W	2-1	Barmby, Mabutt	32,118
23	Jan	9	(a)	Manchester U	L	1-4	Barmby	35,648
24		16	(h)	Sheffield W	L	0-2		25,702
25		27	(h)	Ipswich T	L	0-2		23,738
26		30	(a)	Crystal Palace	W	3-1	Sheringham 2, Gray	20,937
27	Feb	7	(h)	Southampton	W	4-2	Sheringham 2, Anderton, Barmby	20,098
28		10	(a)	Everton	W	2-1	Mabutt, Allen	16,164
29		20	(h)	Leeds U	W	4-0	Ruddock, Sheringham 3 (1 pen)	32,040
30		27	(h)	Queen's Park R	W	3-2	Sheringham 2, Anderton	32,341
31	Mar	2	(a)	Sheffield U	L	0-6		16,654
32		10	(a)	Aston Villa	D	0-0		37,727
33		20	(a)	Chelsea	D	1-1	Sheringham (pen)	25,157
34		24	(h)	Manchester C	W	3-1	Anderton, Nayim, Turner	27,247
35	Apr	9	(h)	Norwich C	W	5-1	Sheringham 2, Allen, Nayim, Ruddock	31,425
36		12	(a)	Nottingham F	L	1-2	Sedgley	25,682
37		17	(h)	Oldham A	W	4-1	Sheringham 2 (2 pens), Turner, Anderton	26,663
38		20	(a)	Middlesbrough	L	0-3		13,472
39	May	1	(h)	Wimbledon	D	1-1	Anderton	24,473
40		5	(h)	Blackburn R	L	1-2	Anderton	23,097
41		8	(a)	Liverpool	L	2-6	Sedgley, Sheringham	43,385
42		11	(a)	Arsenal	W	3-1	Sheringham, Hendry 2	26,393

FINAL LEAGUE POSITION: 8th in F.A. Premier League

Appearances

Sub. Appearances

Goals

Match	Walker	Fenwick	Edinburgh	Howells	Cundy	Ruddock	Turner	Durie	Samways	Anderton	Allen	Gray	Thorstvedt	Sedgley	Tuttle	Hendry	Austin	Sheringham	Van den Hauwe	Watson	Barmby	Nayim	Mabbutt	Moran	Campbell	Bergsson	Nethercott	Hill	Dearden	Hodges	McDonald	Match
1	1	2	3	4	5	6	7*	8	9	10	11	12																				1
2	1†	2	3	4	5*	6	7	8	9	10	11	12	13																			2
3		2†	3			6		8	9	10	11	12	1	4	5	7*	13															3
4			3	4	5	6		8	9	10	11		1			7	2															4
5	1		3		5	6		8	9	7	11*	12				4	2	10														5
6	1				5	6	13	8	9†	7*	11	12				4	2	10	3													6
7	1				5		12	8	9	7*	11	4				6	2	10	3													7
8	1				5	6	12	8	9†	7*	11	4	13				2	10	3													8
9	1				5	6	9	8			11	4†		7	12	13	2*	10	3													9
10	1	12			5		4†			9	11			7	6		2*	10	3	13	8											10
11	1	12	2*		5	6	13			9†	11			7†				10	3		8											11
12	1	2				6		8	4	9†	11			7	5*			10	3	13	12											12
13	1*	2				6		8†	4		11		12	7			3	10			13	9	5									13
14		2	12			6	13	8			11		1	7			3*	10			4†	9	5									14
15		2	7			6		8	4		11		1				3	10				9	5									15
16		2	7	13	6			8*	4		11†		1				3	10			12	9	5									16
17		2	7*	12	6				4				1				3	10	11†		8	9	5	13								17
18			3	7	6				4	12			1				2	10	11†		8*	9	5		13							18
19			3	7	6		8*	4			11		1				2	10			12	9	5									19
20			3	7	6		8	4			11		1				2	10			12	9*	5									20
21			3	7	6			4	9		11		1				2	10			8*		5	12								21
22			3	7	6			4	9*		11		1				2	10			8†		5	12	13							22
23			3	7	6			4	12		11		1				2†	10			8	9*	5		13							23
24			3†	7*	6			4	9		11		1			13	2	10			8		5		12							24
25			3	12	6		8*	4	9		11		1				2†	10	13		7		5									25
26			3	7	6			4	9		11	8*	1				2	10	12				5									26
27			3	7*	6			4	9		11	12	1				2	10	13		8†		5									27
28			3	7	6			4	9		11	8*	1				2†	10	13			12	5									28
29			3	7*	6			4	9		11	12	1				2†	10	13		8†		5									29
30			3		6			4	9		11	7	1				2	10			8*	12	5									30
31					6			4	9		11	7*	1	12		13	2	10	3		8†		5									31
32			3		6	12		4	9		11*	1	7				2	10			8		5									32
33			3		6	11†			9		4	1	7				2	10	7*		8	12	5		13							33
34					6†	13		4	9*	11		1	7				2	10	3		8		5		12							34
35			3		6	13			9†	11		1	7				2	10		4*	8		5		12							35
36			3		6	13			9	11	1*	7					2	10		4	8†		5							12		36
37	1		3		6	12		4*	9	11			7				2	10			8		5									37
38	1	13	3		6	12		4	9	11*			7				2†	10			8		5									38
39	1				6	8		4	9	11*	12		7					10	3				5			2†			13			39
40	1				6	8†		4	9	11			7					10	3				5			2*		12	13			40
41	1				6			9	11			7						10	3*	8†			5				12	4	13		2	41
42	1				6			9	11			7	8*					10	3				5				4		12		2	42
	17	3	31	16	13	38	7	17	34	32	38	9	25	20	4	2	33	38	13	4	17	15	29			3	2		2			
		2	1	2	2		11		2		8		2	1	3	1		5	1	5	3		3	1	5	2	2	1	4			
				1	1	3	3	3		5	5	1		3		2		21		1	5	3	2		1							

1993-94

1	Aug	14	(a)	Newcastle U	W	1-0	Sheringham		34,565
2		16	(h)	Arsenal	L	0-1			28,355
3		21	(h)	Manchester C	W	1-0	Sedgley		24,535
4		25	(a)	Liverpool	W	2-1	Sheringham 2 (1 pen)		42,456
5		28	(a)	Aston Villa	L	0-1			32,498
6	Sep	1	(h)	Chelsea	D	1-1	Sheringham (pen)		27,567
7		11	(a)	Sheffield U	D	2-2	Sheringham 2		21,325
8		18	(h)	Oldham A	W	5-0	Sheringham 2, Sedgley, Durie, Dozzell		24,614
9		26	(a)	Ipswich T	D	2-2	Sheringham, Dozzell		19,437
10	Oct	3	(h)	Everton	W	3-2	Sheringham, Anderton, Caskey		27,487
11		16	(a)	Manchester U	L	1-2	Caskey		44,655
12		23	(h)	Swindon T	D	1-1	Dozzell		31,394
13		30	(a)	Blackburn R	L	0-1			17,462
14	Nov	6	(a)	Southampton	L	0-1			16,017
15		20	(h)	Leeds U	D	1-1	Anderton		31,275
16		24	(h)	Wimbledon	D	1-1	Barmby		17,744
17		27	(a)	Queen's Park R	D	1-1	Anderton		17,694
18	Dec	4	(h)	Newcastle U	L	1-2	Barmby (pen)		30,780
19		6	(a)	Arsenal	D	1-1	Anderton		35,669
20		11	(a)	Manchester C	W	2-0	Dozzell 2		21,566
21		18	(h)	Liverpool	D	3-3	Samways, Hazard (pen), Caskey		31,394
22		27	(h)	Norwich C	L	1-3	Barmby		31,130
23		28	(a)	West Ham U	W	3-1	Dozzell, Hazard, Anderton		20,787
24	Jan	1	(h)	Coventry C	L	1-2	Caskey		26,015
25		3	(a)	Sheffield W	L	0-1			32,514
26		15	(h)	Manchester U	L	0-1			31,343
27		22	(a)	Swindon T	L	1-2	Barmby		16,464
28	Feb	5	(h)	Sheffield W	L	1-3	Rosenthal		23,078
29		12	(h)	Blackburn R	L	0-2			30,236
30		27	(a)	Chelsea	L	3-4	Sedgley, Dozzell, Gray (pen)		19,398
31	Mar	2	(h)	Aston Villa	D	1-1	Rosenthal		17,452
32		5	(h)	Sheffield U	D	2-2	Scott, Dozzell		25,741
33		19	(h)	Ipswich T	D	1-1	Barmby		26,653
34		26	(a)	Everton	W	1-0	Sedgley		23,460
35	Apr	2	(a)	Norwich C	W	2-1	Sheringham, Woodthorpe (og)		21,181
36		4	(h)	West Ham U	L	1-4	Sheringham (pen)		31,502
37		9	(a)	Coventry C	L	0-1			14,487
38		17	(a)	Leeds U	L	0-2			33,658
39		23	(h)	Southampton	W	3-0	Sedgley, Samways, Anderton		25,959
40		30	(a)	Wimbledon	L	1-2	Sheringham (pen)		20,875
41	May	5	(a)	Oldham A	W	2-0	Samways, Howells		14,283
42		7	(h)	Queen's Park R	L	1-2	Sheringham		26,105

FINAL LEAGUE POSITION: 15th in the F.A. Premiership

Appearances

Sub. Appearances

Goals

Thorstvedt	Austin	Campbell	Samways	Calderwood	Mabbutt	Sedgley	Durie	Dozzell	Sheringham	Howells	Turner	Caskey	Anderton	Allen	Moran	Carr	Kerslake	Hill	Barmby	Edinburgh	Robinson	Hendry	Hazard	Nethercott	Walker	Mahorn	Scott	Rosenthal	Gray	#
1	2	3	4	5	6	7	8*	9	10	11	12																			1
1	2	3	4	5	6	7	8	9	10	11*		12																		2
1	2	3	4	5	6	7	8*	9	10	11†		12	14																	3
1	2	3	4	5	6	7	8	9	10	11*		12																		4
1	?	3	4	5	6	7	8	9	10	11*		12†	14																	5
1	2	3*	4	5	6	7	8	9	10	12		11																		6
1	2	3*	4	5	6	7	8	9	10			11	12																	7
1	2*	3	4	5†	6	7	8	9	10			12	11	14																8
1		3	4	5	6	7	8	9	10			12	11			2*														9
1		3†	4	5	6	7		9	10			8	11		12		2	14*												10
1		3	4		6	7		9	10*	5		11			12†		2	8	14											11
1		3	4	5	6	7		9	10†			11			12		2	14	8*											12
1		3		5	6	4		9	10			11*			12			8	2	7†	14									13
1		3	4	5	6	7		9*				12	11					8	2			10								14
1		3	4	5	6	7	8		12				9					10*	2			11								15
1		3	4	5	6*	7			10			12	9					8	2			11								16
1		3	4	5	6	7*			10				9					8	2		12†	11	14							17
1	14	11*	4	5	6				12			10	9			2†			8	3		7								18
1	12	11	4*	5	6				10			7†	9			2				3	14	8								19
1		11	4	5	6				10			7	9			2				3		8								20
1			4	5	6				10			7	9			2			8	3		11								21
1			4	5	6				10			7	9			2			8	3		11								22
1		12	4	5	6				10			7	9			2			8*	3		11								23
1		12	4	5	6				10			7	9			2			8	3		11*								24
1		12	4	5	6				10			7	9			2			8*	3		11								25
	12	11	4	5	6				10				9			2			8†	3*	14	7			1					26
1†	2	12	4	5	6							7	9*						8	3				10	14	11				27
	2		4		6							7*	9						8	3				10	1		5	11	12	28
	2		4		6							7	9						8	3				10	1		5	11		29
	2	12	4		6	7		10†					9							3*			8		1		5	11	14	30
	2	3	4		6	7			10				9						8						1		5	11		31
	2*	3	4		6	7			10			12	9						8						1		5	11		32
	2*	3			6	4			10			7	9		12				8						1		5	11		33
	12		4		6	7		14					9			2			8	3*				10	1		5†	11		34
		3	4		6	7		10	12				9			2			8						1		5	11*		35
		3	4		6	7		10†	12	14			9			2			8						1		5	11*		36
1		3*	4		6	7		14	10	11†			9			2			8								5	12		37
1	2	12			6	4†	8		10	11			9*							3			14				5	7		38
1	2	4*		5	6				10	11†			9						8	3			14		7			12		39
1	2	4		5*	6				10	11			9†						8	3			14		7			12		40
1	2	4			6	7	12		10	11										3			8				5	9*		41
1	2	4		5	6				10				9				11†	8*		3			14		7			12		42
32	20	27	39	26	29	42	10	28	17	15		16	35		1	16	1	27	24	1		13	9	10	1	12	11			
	3	7				4	2	3	1	9		2	1	5		1	2		1	1	3	4	1	1				4	2	
		3				5	1	8	14	1		4	6						5			2					1	2	1	

65

1994-95

#	Month	Date		Opponent	Result		Scorers	Attendance
1	Aug	20	(a)	Sheffield W	W	4-3	Sheringham, Anderton, Barmby, Klinsmann	34,051
2		24	(h)	Everton	W	2-1	Klinsmann 2	24,553
3		27	(h)	Manchester U	L	0-1		24,502
4		30	(a)	Ipswich T	W	3-1	Klinsmann 2, Dumitrescu	22,430
5	Sep	12	(h)	Southampton	L	1-2	Klinsmann	22,387
6		17	(a)	Leicester C	L	1-3	Klinsmann	21,300
7		24	(h)	Nottingham F	L	1-4	Dumitrescu	24,558
8	Oct	1	(a)	Wimbledon	W	2-1	Sheringham, Popescu	16,802
9		8	(h)	Queen's Park R	D	1-1	Barmby	25,799
10		15	(a)	Leeds U	D	1-1	Sheringham	39,362
11		22	(a)	Manchester C	L	2-5	Dumitrescu 2 (1 pen)	25,473
12		29	(h)	West Ham U	W	3-1	Klinsmann, Sheringham, Barmby	26,271
13	Nov	5	(a)	Blackburn R	L	0-2		26,933
14		19	(h)	Aston Villa	L	3-4	Sheringham, Klinsmann (pen), Bosnich (og)	26,889
15		23	(h)	Chelsea	D	0-0		27,037
16		26	(a)	Liverpool	D	1-1	Ruddock (og)	35,007
17	Dec	3	(h)	Newcastle U	W	4-2	Sheringham 3, Popescu	28,002
18		10	(h)	Sheffield W	W	3-1	Barmby, Klinsmann, Calderwood	25,912
19		17	(a)	Everton	D	0-0		32,813
20		26	(a)	Norwich C	W	2-0	Barmby, Sheringham	21,814
21		27	(h)	Crystal Palace	D	0-0		27,730
22		31	(a)	Coventry C	W	4-0	Darby (og), Barmby, Anderton, Sheringham	19,965
23	Jan	2	(h)	Arsenal	W	1-0	Popescu	28,747
24		14	(a)	West Ham U	W	2-1	Sheringham	24,578
25		25	(a)	Aston Villa	L	0-1		40,017
26	Feb	5	(h)	Blackburn R	W	3-1	Klinsmann, Anderton, Barmby	28,124
27		11	(a)	Chelsea	D	1-1	Sheringham	30,812
28		25	(h)	Wimbledon	L	1-2	Klinsmann	27,258
29	Mar	4	(a)	Nottingham F	D	2-2	Sheringham, Calderwood	28,711
30		8	(h)	Ipswich T	W	3-0	Klinsmann, Barmby, Youds (og)	24,930
31		15	(a)	Manchester U	D	0-0		43,802
32		18	(h)	Leicester C	W	1-0	Klinsmann	30,851
33		22	(h)	Liverpool	D	0-0		31,988
34	Apr	2	(a)	Southampton	L	3-4	Sheringham 2, Klinsmann	15,105
35		11	(h)	Manchester C	W	2-1	Howells, Klinsmann	27,410
36		14	(a)	Crystal Palace	D	1-1	Klinsmann	18,068
37		17	(h)	Norwich C	W	1-0	Sheringham	32,304
38		29	(a)	Arsenal	D	1-1	Klinsmann	38,337
39	May	3	(a)	Newcastle U	D	3-3	Barmby, Klinsmann, Anderton	35,603
40		6	(a)	Queen's Park R	L	1-2	Sheringham	18,637
41		9	(h)	Coventry C	L	1-3	Anderton	24,930
42		14	(h)	Leeds U	D	1-1	Sheringham	33,040

FINAL LEAGUE POSITION: 7th in the F.A. Premiership

Appearances

Sub. Appearances

Goals

Walker	Kerslake	Edinburgh	Nethercott	Calderwood	Cambell	Anderton	Barmby	Klinsmann	Sheringham	Dumitrescu	Hazzard	Mabbutt	Popescu	Hill	Scott	Dozzell	Austin	Rosenthal	Thorstvedt	Howells	Caskey	McMahon	Turner	
1	2	3	4	5	6†	7	8	9	10	11*		12	14											1
1	2	3	4†	5	6	7	8	9	10	11*		12	14											2
1	2	3	4	5*	6	7	8	9	10	11		12												3
1	2	3	4*	5	6	7	8	9	10	11		12												4
1	2	3	4	5	6	7	8*	9	10	11		12												5
1	2	3	4	5*	6	7	8	9	10	11		12												6
1	2	3		5		7		9	10	11	8*	6	4	12										7
1	2					7		9	10	11*	12	6	4		5	8	3							8
1	2	3	4*	6			8	9	10	12			11		5	7†	14							9
1	2	3	12	6*			8	9	10	11			4		5	7								10
1	2	3		6			8	9	10	11		12	4		5	7*								11
	2	3*		5			8	9	12	11		6	4		7†		14		1	10				12
1	2	3		5			8	9	10	12		6*	4				11†	14		7				13
1	2†		14	5	3	7	12	9	10			6	4							11	8*			14
1				5	3	7	8*	9	10	12		6	4				2			11				15
1				5	3	7*	8	9	10	12		6	4				2			11				16
1	12			5	3	7*	8	9	10			6	4				2			11				17
1				5	3	7	8	9	10			6	4				2	4		11				18
1				5	3	7	8		10			6	4				2	9		11				19
1	12			5	3	7	8	9	10			6	4				2			11*				20
1	12			5	3	7	8†	9	10			6	4				2	14		11*				21
1			14	5	3	7	8*	9	10			6	4†				2	12		11				22
1	12			5	3	7		9	10			6	4*				2	8		11				23
1	12			5	3*	7	8	9	10			6	4				2			11				24
1		3		5	11	7	8	9*	10			6	4				2			12				25
1		3	12	5	2	7	8*	9	10			6	4							11				26
1		3		5	2	7	8	9	10			6	4							11				27
1		3		5	2*	7	8	9	10			6	4†			12	14			11				28
1		3		5		7	8	9	10			6					2	4		11				29
1		3		5		7	8	9	10			6					2	4*		11		12		30
1		3		5		7	8	9	10			6					2	4		11				31
1		3		5		7	8	9	10			6					2	4		11				32
1	12	3	4*			7	8	9	10			6					2			11		5		33
1		3		5		7	8	9	10			6					2	4		11				34
1		3	12	5		7	8*	9	10			6	4				2	14		11†				35
1		3		5		7	8	9	10			6	4				2			11				36
1		3		5		7	8*	9	10			6	4				2	12		11				37
1		3		5		7	8	9	10			6					2	4		11				38
1		3		5	12	7	8*	9	10			6					2	4		11				39
1	12	3	14	5	2	7	8†	9	10			6						4		11*				40
1		3	12	5	2*	7	8	9	10			6						4		11				41
1	2	3	4	5		7		9	10			6	12							11*		8		42
41	16	29	8	35	29	37	37	41	41	11	2	33	23	1	4	6	23	14	1	26	1	2	1	
	2	2	9	1	1		1			1		2	9	3			2	1		1	6	3		
			2			5	9	20	18	4			3					1						

1995-96

								Scorers	Attendance
1	Aug	19	(a)	Manchester C	D	1-1		Sheringham	30,827
2		23	(h)	Aston Villa	L	0-1			26,598
3		26	(h)	Liverpool	L	1-3		Barnes (og)	31,254
4		30	(a)	West Ham U	D	1-1		Rosenthal	23,516
5	Sep	9	(h)	Leeds U	W	2-1		Howells, Sheringham	30,034
6		16	(a)	Sheffield W	W	3-1		Sheringham 2 (1 pen), Walker (og)	26,565
7		25	(a)	Queen's Park R	W	3-2		Sheringham 2 (1 pen), Dozzell	15,659
8		30	(h)	Wimbledon	W	3-1		Sheringham 2, Elkins (og)	25,321
9	Oct	14	(h)	Nottingham F	L	0-1			32,876
10		22	(a)	Everton	D	1-1		Armstrong	33,629
11		29	(h)	Newcastle U	D	1-1		Armstrong	32,257
12	Nov	4	(a)	Coventry C	W	3-2		Fox, Sheringham, Howells	17,567
13		18	(h)	Arsenal	W	2-1		Sheringham, Armstrong	32,894
14		21	(a)	Middlesbrough	W	1-0		Armstrong	29,487
15		25	(a)	Chelsea	D	0-0			31,059
16	Dec	2	(h)	Everton	D	0-0			32,894
17		9	(h)	Queen's Park R	W	1-0		Sheringham	28,851
18		16	(a)	Wimbledon	W	1-0		Fox	16,193
19		23	(h)	Bolton W	D	2-2		Sheringham, Armstrong	30,702
20		26	(a)	Southampton	D	0-0			15,238
21		30	(a)	Blackburn R	L	1-2		Sheringham	30,004
22	Jan	1	(h)	Manchester U	W	4-1		Sheringham, Campbell, Armstrong 2	32,852
23		13	(h)	Manchester C	W	1-0		Armstrong	31,438
24		21	(a)	Aston Villa	L	1-2		Fox	35,666
25	Feb	3	(a)	Liverpool	D	0-0			40,628
26		142	(h)	West Ham U	L	0-1			29,781
27		24	(h)	Sheffield W	W	1-0		Armstrong	32,047
28	Mar	2	(h)	Southampton	W	1-0		Dozzell	26,320
29		16	(h)	Blackburn R	L	2-3		Sheringham, Armstrong	31,803
30		20	(a)	Bolton W	W	3-2		Howells, Fox, Armstrong	17,829
31		24	(a)	Manchester U	L	0-1			50,508
32		30	(h)	Coventry C	W	3-1		Sheringham, Fox 2	26,808
33	Apr	6	(a)	Nottingham F	L	1-2		Armstrong	27,053
34		8	(h)	Middlesbrough	D	1-1		Armstrong	32,036
35		15	(a)	Arsenal	D	0-0			38,273
36		27	(h)	Chelsea	D	1-1		Armstrong	32,918
37	May	2	(a)	Leeds U	W	3-1		Armstrong, Anderton 2	30,024
38		5	(a)	Newcastle U	D	1-1		Dozzell	36,589

FINAL LEAGUE POSITION: 8th in the F.A. Premiership

Appearances

Sub. Appearances

Goals

The table below records the squad-number worn by each player in each League match (numbered 1–38 in the right-hand column), with * and † denoting substitutions. The three rows at the foot give total starts, substitute appearances and goals.

Walker	Austin	Edinburgh	Nethercott	Howells	Mabbutt	Kerslake	Dumitrescu	Armstrong	Sheringham	Rosenthal	Scott	Calderwood	McMahon	Wilson	Dozzell	Anderton	Campbell	Fox	Slade	Caskey	Sinton	Cundy	
1	2	3*	4	5	6	7	8	9	10	11	12												1
1	2	3		4	6	7*	8	9	10	11		5	12										2
1		2		4	6		8	9	10	11		5	7*	3	12								3
1	?			4	6			9	10	11		5	7*	3	8	12							4
1	2			4†	6			9	10	11	12	5	13	3	8	7*							5
1	2	12			6			9	10	11		5	8	3		7	4*						6
1	2	12		4	6			9	10	11		5		3	8	7*							7
1	2		4*	6				9	10	11		5	8	3	12		7						8
1	2			4	6				10	11		5	8	3	12	7*	9						9
1	2			4	6			9	10	11		5	8*	3	13	7†	11						10
1	2			4	6			9	10	11†		12	13	3	8	5*	7						11
1	2			4	6			9	10	11*		12		3	8	5	7						12
1	2			4	6			9	10	11*		5	12		8	3	7						13
1	2			4	6			9	10	11		5			8	3	7						14
1	2			4	6			9	10	11*		5	12		8	3	7						15
1	2			4	6			9	10	11*		5	12		8	3	7						16
1		12		4	6			9	10	11		5		3	8	2*	7						17
1		12		4	6			9	10	11		5		3	8*	2†	7	13					18
1		3	12	4*	6			9	10	8		5		11		2	7						19
1	2	3			6			9	10	8		5	4*	11			7		12				20
1	2	3	4		6		8	9	10	7		5				11							21
1	2	3	4			8*	9	10	11		5	12			6		7						22
1	2	3	4		6			9	10	11				8		5		7					23
1	2	3	4					9	10	11		5				6	7	8					24
1	2	3	12		6			9	10	13		5		8		4*	7				11†		25
1	2				6			9	10	11*		5		3	8	4	7				12		26
1				4	6			9	10	12		5		3	8	2	7*				11		27
1				4	6				10	12		5		3	8	2	7	9*			11		28
1	2	3	4	6				9	10			5*		8			7				11	12	29
1	2	12		4	6			9	10			5*		3	8	11	7†	13					30
1	2		12	4	6*			9	10					3	8	5	7				11		31
1	2			4	6			9	10					3	8	5	7				11		32
1	2	12		4	6*			9	10	13				3	8	5	7				11†		33
1	2	12		4	6*			9	10†	11				3	8	5	7	13					34
1		2	12	4	6			9	10	11				3	8†	13	5*	7					35
1		2			6			9	10	12				3	8	7	5	4			11*		36
1		2		4	6			9	10					3	8	7	5	11					37
1		2		4	6			9	10	12		13		3	8	7	5†	11*					38
38	28	15	9	29	32	2	5	36	38	29		26	7	28	24	6	31	26	1	3	8		
	7	4							7	2	3	7		4	2			4		1	1		
				3				15	16	1					3	2	1	6					

69

1996-97

#	Month	Date		Opponent	Result	Score	Scorers	Attendance
1	Aug	17	(a)	Blackburn R	W	2-0	Armstrong 2	26,960
2		21	(h)	Derby Co	D	1-1	Sheringham	28,219
3		24	(h)	Everton	D	0-0		29,669
4	Sep	4	(a)	Wimbledon	L	0-1		17,306
5		7	(h)	Newcastle U	L	1-2	Allen	32,594
6		14	(a)	Southampton	W	1-0	Armstrong (pen)	15,251
7		22	(h)	Leicester C	L	1-2	Wilson (pen)	24,159
8		29	(a)	Manchester U	L	0-2		54,943
9	Oct	12	(h)	Aston Villa	W	1-0	Nielsen	32,840
10		19	(a)	Middlesbrough	W	3-0	Sheringham 2, Fox	30,215
11		26	(a)	Chelsea	L	1-3	Armstrong	28,318
12	Nov	2	(h)	West Ham U	W	1-0	Armstrong	32,975
13		16	(h)	Sunderland	W	2-0	Sinton, Sheringham	31,867
14		24	(a)	Arsenal	L	1-3	Sinton	38,264
15	Dec	2	(h)	Liverpool	L	0-2		32,899
16		7	(a)	Coventry C	W	2-1	Sheringham, Sinton	19,656
17		14	(a)	Leeds U	D	0-0		33,783
18		21	(h)	Sheffield W	D	1-1	Nielsen	30,996
19		26	(h)	Southampton	W	3-1	Iversen 2, Nielsen	30,549
20		28	(a)	Newcastle U	L	1-7	Nielsen	36,308
21	Jan	12	(h)	Manchester U	L	1-2	Allen	33,026
22		19	(a)	Nottingham F	L	1-2	Sinton	27,303
23		29	(h)	Blackburn R	W	2-1	Iversen, Sinton	22,943
24	Feb	1	(h)	Chelsea	L	1-2	Howells	33,027
25		15	(h)	Arsenal	D	0-0		33,039
26		24	(a)	West Ham U	L	3-4	Sheringham, Anderton, Howells	23,998
27	Mar	1	(h)	Nottingham F	L	0-1		32,805
28		4	(a)	Sunderland	W	4-0	Iversen 3, Nielsen	20,729
29		15	(h)	Leeds U	W	1-0	Anderton	33,040
30		19	(a)	Leicester C	D	1-1	Sheringham	20,593
31		22	(a)	Derby Co	L	2-4	Rosenthal, Dozzell	18,083
32	Apr	5	(h)	Wimbledon	W	1-0	Dozzell	32,654
33		9	(a)	Sheffield W	L	1-2	Nielsen	22,671
34		12	(a)	Everton	L	0-1		36,380
35		19	(a)	Aston Villa	D	1-1	Vega	39,339
36		24	(h)	Middlesbrough	W	1-0	Sinton	29,940
37	May	3	(a)	Liverpool	L	1-2	Anderton	40,003
38		11	(h)	Coventry C	L	1-2	McVeigh	33,029

FINAL LEAGUE POSITION: 10th in the F.A. Premiership

Appearances

Sub. Appearances

Goals

Walker	Campbell	Edinburgh	Howells	Calderwood	Mabbutt	Anderton	Fox	Armstrong	Sheringham	Sinton	Nethercott	Wilson	Dozzell	Rosenthal	Nielsen	Allen	Carr	Iversen	Scales	Vega	Austin	Fenn	McVeigh	Baardsen	Clapham	No.
1	2	3	4	5	6*	7°	8	9	10	11	12†	13	14													1
1	6	2	4	5		7†	8*	9	10	11		3	12	13												2
1	6	2	4	5		7	9*	10	11			3	8	12												3
1	6	2	4	5		7*	10			11	12	3	9†	13	8°	14										4
1	6	2	4	5		7*	12	9		11		3		13	8	10†										5
1	6	2	4	5		7†	12	9		11*	14	3		13	8°	10										6
1	9	2*	4	5		7	11			12	6	3		13	8†	10										7
1	6	12	4*	5		7†			10	11		3		13	8	9	2									8
1	6	12	4	5		7	9	10	11*	13		3			8†		2									9
1	6	3	4	5		7	9	10		11					8		2									10
1	6	3	4	5		7*	9	10		11	12				8†	13	2									11
1	6	3	4	5			9	10		11				12	8	7*	2									12
1	6		4	5		7*		9	10	11		3		12	8		2									13
1	6		4	5		7		9	10	11		3			8		2									14
1	6	12	4	5		7	9†	10	11*			3			8	13	2									15
1	6		4	5		7			10	11		3	12		8*		2	9								16
1	6		4	5		7			10	11		3			8		2	9								17
1	6*		4	5		7			10	11		3			8		2	9	12							18
1	6		4	5		7*			10	11		3			8		2	9	12							19
1	6		4	5		7			10	11*		3	12†	13	8		2	9								20
1	6	3	8	5		12			7			11				10	2*	9		4†	13					21
1	6	3	8	5*					11†	12	14			13	10	7°	2	9		4						22
1	6	3	4			12	7*			11	13				8	10	2	9		5†						23
1	5	3°	4			12	14			11	6†	13			8	10	7*	9			2					24
1	6	3	8	5		7			10						11		2	9		4						25
1	6		8†	5		7			10	11*		3		13	12		2	9		4						26
1	6		8	5					10	11†		3	13	12	7			9	4		2*					27
1	6		8	5		7			10			3*			11	12		9	4		2					28
1	6			5		7			10	11					8	12	2	9*	4		3					29
1	6		8*	5					10	11				12	13	7	2	9	4		3†					30
1	6			5					10	11*				8	12	7	2	9	4		3					31
1	6	3				7			10	11				8	9	5			4		2					32
1	5*	3	12			7	8°		10	11					9	6†	13		4		2	14				33
1	11	3		5			12		10					8	9	7†	2*		4°	6	13	14				34
1	6	3	7*	5					10	11	12		8						4		2	13	9†			35
1	6	3	7	5					10	11			8		9				4		2					36
1°		3	9*	5		7†	12		10	11			8						4	6	2		13	15		37
	6	3				7			10	11†				8			2		4	5	12		9*	1	13	38
37	38	21	32	33	1	14	19	12	29	32	2	23	10	4	28	9	4	16	10	6	13		2	1		
	3		1		2	6			1	7	3	7	16	1	3	2		2		2	2	4	1	1	1	
		2		3	1	5	7	6		1	2	1	6	2		6		1		1						

71

1997-98

#	Month	Date		Opponent	Result	Score	Scorers	Attendance
1	Aug	10	(h)	Manchester U	L	0-2		26,359
2		13	(a)	West Ham U	L	1-2	Ferdinand	25,354
3		23	(h)	Derby Co	W	1-0	Calderwood	25,886
4		27	(h)	Aston Villa	W	3-2	Ferdinand 2, Fox	26,316
5		30	(a)	Arsenal	D	0-0		38,102
6	Sep	13	(a)	Leicester C	L	0-3		20,683
7		20	(h)	Blackburn R	D	0-0		26,573
8		23	(a)	Bolton W	D	1-1	Armstrong	23,433
9		27	(h)	Wimbledon	D	0-0		26,261
10	Oct	4	(a)	Newcastle U	L	0-1		36,708
11		19	(h)	Sheffield W	W	3-2	Dominguez, Armstrong, Ginola	25,097
12		25	(a)	Southampton	L	2-3	Dominguez, Ginola	15,255
13	Nov	1	(h)	Leeds U	L	0-1		26,441
14		8	(a)	Liverpool	L	0-4		38,006
15		24	(h)	Crystal Palace	L	0-1		25,634
16		29	(a)	Everton	W	2-0	Vega, Ginola	36,670
17	Dec	6	(h)	Chelsea	L	1-6	Vega	28,476
18		13	(a)	Coventry C	L	0-4		19,490
19		20	(h)	Barnsley	W	3-0	Nielsen, Ginola 2	28,232
20		26	(a)	Aston Villa	L	1-4	Calderwood	38,644
21		28	(h)	Arsenal	D	1-1	Nielsen	29,601
22	Jan	10	(a)	Manchester U	L	0-2		55,281
23		17	(h)	West Ham U	W	1-0	Klinsmann	30,284
24		31	(a)	Derby Co	L	1-2	Fox	30,187
25	Feb	7	(a)	Blackburn R	W	3-0	Berti, Armstrong, Fox	30,388
26		14	(h)	Leicester C	D	1-1	Calderwood	28,355
27		21	(a)	Sheffield W	L	0-1		29,871
28	Mar	1	(h)	Bolton W	W	1-0	Nielsen	29,032
29		4	(a)	Leeds U	L	0-1		31,802
30		14	(h)	Liverpool	D	3-3	Klinsmann, Ginola, Vega	30,245
31		28	(a)	Crystal Palace	W	3-1	Berti, Armstrong, Klinsmann	26,116
32	Apr	4	(h)	Everton	D	1-1	Armstrong	35,624
33		11	(a)	Chelsea	L	0-2		34,149
34		13	(h)	Coventry C	D	1-1	Berti	33,463
35		18	(a)	Barnsley	D	1-1	Calderwood	18,692
36		25	(h)	Newcastle U	W	2-0	Klinsmann, Ferdinand	35,847
37	May	2	(a)	Wimbledon	W	6-2	Ferdinand, Klinsmann 4, Saib	25,972
38		10	(h)	Southampton	D	1-1	Klinsmann	35,995

FINAL LEAGUE POSITION: 14th in the F.A. Premiership

Appearances

Sub. Appearances

Goals

Walker I	Carr S	Edinburgh J	Clemence S	Vega R	Campbell S	Ginola D	Nielsen A	Iversen S	Ferdinand L	Howells D	Sinton A	Scales J	Dominguez J	Calderwood C	Fox R	Mabbutt G	Fenn N	Armstrong C	Mahorn P	Anderton D	Allen R	Wilson C	Klinsmann J	Baardsen E	Berti N	Brady G	Saib M	
1	2	3	4*	5	6	7	8	9	10	11	12																	1
1	2	3	13	5	6†	7	8*	9	10	11	12	4																2
1	2	3	6			7†	12	9	10	8	11*	4	13	5														3
1	2	3*	6					9	10†	8	11	4		5	7	12	13											4
1	2	3	6		5		12	9°	10	8	11†	4	13		7*	14												5
1	2		3		5	7	8		10*	9		4	11		6		12											6
1	2	3	4	12	5	7			8	11				10	6			9*										7
1	2	3†	8	13	4	7	12					11	5*	10	6				14	9°								8
1	2		3	4	5	7	12		10			11		8*	6			9										9
1	2	8*	4	3	11†			10		12		13	5	7	6			9										10
1	2*	3		5	6	7			4	10		11†	12	8		13°	9			14								11
1	2	3†		5	6	7			4	10		11	13°	8*		14	9			12								12
1	12	2		5	7		13		8°	3	4	11†		10	6*		9			14								13
1	2	3			6	11		9		8	13	4	14	5†		12	7°	10*										14
1	2	3*	6	12	5	11	13	9†	10		8	4				7°	14											15
1	2		4	6*	7	8°	13	10†		11	12			5	9			14		3								16
1	2	12	6		7	8†		10	11*	4°		5	9			13	14	3										17
1	2	12	13		11	4	14	9	10†			5	8	6		7°		3*										18
1	2	12		6	11*	4	13	9†	10		14	5	8			7°		3										19
1	2	12		4	7	8	9		11*			5	10	6†			13	14	3°									20
1	2	10	4	6	11*	8	12					13	5	7†					3	9								21
	2	8*	4	6					12			11	5	7†					3	9	1	10	13					22
	2		4	6	7†				12	11		13	5*	10°					3	9	1	8	14					23
	2		4	5	7			10	12	11*		13		8				3†	9	1	6							24
	2	12	4	5	11	8*		9†	10				7		13				3°		1	6	14					25
	2	12	4	6	11	8						5†	7		9				3*		1	10	13					26
	2	3*		6	11	8		4				12	5	7		9					1	10†	13					27
	2			6	11°	8			12				5	7†		9*				3	10	1	4	13	14			28
	2		5	6	11	8		4°						7	12					3*	9	1	10†	13	14			29
	2		5	6	11†	8			12					7		9*				3	10	1	4	13				30
1	2*		4	6				12				13	5	7°		9†				3	10		8	14	11			31
1	2*		5	6	11	8		12					13	7		9				3†	10		4°	14				32
1	2		5	6	11	3		12					13	7		9*	14				10†		4°		8			33
1	2		5	6	11	3		12					13	7		9*					10		4		8†			34
1	2		4	6	11	3		10*						5	7		13	12			9†		8					35
1	2		5	6	11			10					3	8		7*					9		4		12			36
1	2			6	11	3		10*					5	8†		12	7				9		4		13			37
1	2			6	11	3		10					5*	8	12		7				9		4†		13			38
29	37	13	12	22	34	34	21	8	19	14	14	9	8	21	32	8		13	2	7	1	16	15	9	17		3	
	1	3	5	3		5	5	2	6	5	1	10	5		3	4	6		8	3					9	6		
		3		6	3		5			2	4	3			5					9		3			1			

73

1998-99

#	Month	Date		Opponent	Res	Score	Scorers	Attendance
1	Aug	15	(a)	Wimbledon	L	1-3	Fox	23,031
2		22	(h)	Sheffield Wednesd	L	0-3		32,075
3		29	(a)	Everton	W	1-0	Ferdinand	39,378
4	Sep	9	(h)	Blackburn Rovers	W	2-1	Ferdinand, Nielsen	28,338
5		13	(h)	Middlesbrough	L	0-3		30,437
6		19	(a)	Southampton	D	1-1	Fox	15,204
7		26	(h)	Leeds United	D	3-3	Vega, Iversen, Campbell	35,535
8	Oct	3	(a)	Derby County	W	1-0	Campbell	30,083
9		19	(a)	Leicester City	L	1-2	Ferdinand	20,787
10		24	(h)	Newcastle United	W	2-0	Iversen 2	36,047
11	Nov	2	(h)	Charlton Athletic	D	2-2	Nielsen, Armstrong	32,202
12		7	(a)	Aston Villa	L	2-3	Anderton (pen), Vega	39,241
13		14	(a)	Arsenal	D	0-0		38,278
14		21	(h)	Nottingham Forest	W	2-0	Armstrong, Nielsen	35,832
15		28	(a)	West Ham United	L	1-2	Armstrong	26,044
16	Dec	5	(h)	Liverpool	W	2-1	Fox, Carragher (og)	36,125
17		12	(h)	Manchester United	D	2-2	Campbell 2	36,058
18		19	(a)	Chelsea	L	0-2		34,881
19		26	(a)	Coventry City	D	1-1	Campbell	23,091
20		28	(h)	Everton	W	4-1	Ferdinand, Armstrong 3	36,053
21	Jan	9	(a)	Sheffield Wednesd	D	0-0		28,204
22		16	(h)	Wimbledon	D	0-0		32,422
23		30	(a)	Blackburn Rovers	D	1-1	Iversen	29,643
24	Feb	6	(h)	Coventry City	D	0-0		34,376
25		20	(a)	Middlesbrough	D	0-0		34,687
26		27	(h)	Derby County	D	1-1	Sherwood	35,392
27	Mar	2	(h)	Southampton	W	3-0	Armstrong, Iversen, Dominguez	28,580
28		10	(a)	Leeds United	L	0-2		34,561
29		13	(h)	Aston Villa	W	1-0	Sherwood	35,963
30	Apr	3	(h)	Leicester City	L	0-2		35,415
31		5	(a)	Newcastle United	D	1-1	Anderton (pen)	36,655
32		17	(a)	Nottingham Forest	W	1-0	Iversen	25,181
33		20	(a)	Charlton Athletic	W	4-1	Iversen, Campbell, Dominguez, Ginola	20,043
34		24	(h)	West Ham United	L	1-2	Ginola	36,089
35	May	1	(a)	Liverpool	L	2-3	Carragher (og), Iversen	44,007
36		5	(h)	Arsenal	L	1-3	Anderton	36,019
37		10	(h)	Chelsea	D	2-2	Iversen, Ginola	35,878
38		16	(a)	Manchester United	L	1-2	Ferdinand	55,189

FINAL LEAGUE POSITION: 11th in the F.A. Premiership

Appearances

Sub. Appearances

Goals

Walker IM	Carr S	Tramezzani P	Berti N	Vega R	Campbell SJ	Fox RA	Anderton DR	Armstrong CP	Ferdinand L	Ginola DDM	Nielsen A	Saib M	Dominguez JMM	Baardsen PE	Calderwood C	Clemence SN	Sinton A	Segers JCA	Edinburgh JC	Iversen S	Scales JR	Allen R	Young LP	Freund S	Taricco MR	Sherwood TA	Nilsen R	King L	
1	2	3	4*	5	6	7	8†	9	10	11	12	13																	1
1	2	3†		5*	6	7	8	9	10	11	4	12	13																2
	2	3		5	6	7	8	12	9*	11	10			1	4														3
	2	3	4	5		7			9	11†	10	12		1	6	8*	13												4
	2	3	4		6	7°		13	9	11	10†	14		1	5	8*	12												5
	2	3	8*	5	6	7			9	11		12		4	10			1											6
	2*			5	6	7	11	9	10°		4		13	1	12	8†			3	14									7
	2			5	6	7†	8	13	9	11*	10			1	4	12			3										8
	2			5	6	7	8	13	9	11*		12		1	4	10†			3										9
	2				6		7	9	10†	11*	8			1	4	13			3	12	5								10
	2				6		7†	8	9		10			1	4	13	11*		3		5	12							11
	2			12	6		7†	8		11	4			1	10°		13		3*	9	5	14							12
	2			4	6	7		9		11				1	8*		12		3	10	5								13
	2				6	7	9°		11	8			1	4*	13	12			3†	10	5	14							14
	2				6	7	12	9		11	4			1	8*				3	10	5								15
1	2				6	7	8	9	12	11	4								3	10*			5						16
1	2				6	7*	8	9	10	11	4								3	12			5						17
1	2				6	7°	8	9	10	11	4					14			3†	12		13	5						18
1	2				6	7	8	9	10†	11*	4								3	12		13	5						19
1	2				6	7	8	9†	10	11	4*								3	12		13	5						20
1	2				6	7†	13	10*	11°	8	12								3	9		14	5	4					21
1	2			12	6		13	9	11	5*	8°					7†			3	10		14	4						22
1	2			5	6	7	12	10	8	11*									3	9				4					23
1	2				6	7	13	10	8	11	9*												5	4	3†	12			24
1	2			5	6	7	12	10*		11	9													4	3	8			25
1				5	6	7	12	9*		11										10				4	2	8			26
1	2			12	6	7	13	9		11†										10			5*	4	3	8			27
1	2				6	7†	13	9		11°	12									10*		14	5	4	3	8			28
1	2			5	6	7		9†	10	11°	4									12		13			3*	8			29
1	2				6	7*	13	10	8	11	12								3†	9			5	4					30
1	2				6	7		9		11										10					3	8	5		31
1	2				6	7	12	9		11										10*			5	4	3	8			32
1	2				6	7	12	9†		11										10		13		4*	3	8	5		33
1	2				6	7†	13	9*		11	12									10			5	4	3	8			34
1	2		14		6	7		9		11*						8°				10				4†	3	13	5	12	35
1	2				6	7	13	9		11†										10		12	5	4	3*	8			36
1	2				6	7	13	9		11†										10		12	5	4*	3	8			37
1	2				6	7	13†		10	11*										9		14	5°	4	3	8		12	38
25	37	6	4	13	37	17	31	24	22	30	24		2	12	11	9	12	1	14	22	7		14	17	12	12	3		
			3		3	1	10	2		4	4		11		1	9	10		2	5		5	1		1	2	1		
			2		6	3	3	7	5	3	3		2							9						2			

75

1999-2000

#	Month	Date		Opponent		Score	Scorers	Attendance
1	Aug	7	(a)	West Ham United	L	0-1		26,010
2		9	(h)	Newcastle United	W	3-1	Iversen, Ferdinand, Sherwood	28,701
3		14	(h)	Everton	W	3-2	Sherwood, Leonhardsen, Iversen	34,308
4		21	(a)	Sheffield Wednesd	W	2-1	Ferdinand, Leonhardsen	24,027
5		28	(h)	Leeds United	L	1-2	Sherwood	36,012
6	Sep	12	(a)	Bradford City	D	1-1	Perry	18,143
7		19	(h)	Coventry City	W	3-2	Iversen, Armstrong, Leonhardsen	35,224
8		26	(a)	Wimbledon	D	1-1	Carr	17,368
9	Oct	3	(h)	Leicester City	L	2-3	Iversen 2	35,591
10		16	(a)	Derby County	W	1-0	Armstrong	29,815
11		23	(h)	Manchester United	W	3-1	Iversen, Scholes (og), Carr	36,072
12		31	(a)	Sunderland	L	1-2	Iversen	41,042
13	Nov	7	(h)	Arsenal	W	2-1	Iversen, Sherwood	36,085
14		20	(a)	Southampton	W	1-0	Leonhardsen	15,248
15		28	(a)	Newcastle United	L	1-2	Armstrong	36,454
16	Dec	6	(h)	West Ham United	D	0-0		36,233
17		18	(a)	Middlesbrough	L	1-2	Vega	33,113
18		26	(h)	Watford	W	4-0	Ginola, Iversen, Sherwood 2	36,089
19		29	(a)	Aston Villa	D	1-1	Sherwood	39,217
20	Jan	3	(h)	Liverpool	W	1-0	Armstrong	36,044
21		12	(a)	Chelsea	L	0-1		34,969
22		15	(a)	Everton	D	2-2	Armstrong, Watson (og)	36,144
23		22	(h)	Sheffield Wednesd	L	0-1		35,897
24	Feb	5	(h)	Chelsea	L	0-1		36,041
25		12	(a)	Leeds United	L	0-1		40,127
26		26	(a)	Coventry City	W	1-0	Armstrong	23,073
27	Mar	4	(h)	Bradford City	D	1-1	Iversen	35,472
28		11	(h)	Southampton	W	7-2	Richards (og), Anderton, Armstrong 2, Iversen 3	36,024
29		19	(a)	Arsenal	L	1-2	Armstrong	38,131
30		25	(a)	Watford	D	1-1	Armstrong	20,050
31	Apr	3	(h)	Middlesbrough	L	2-3	Armstrong, Ginola	31,804
32		9	(a)	Liverpool	L	0-2		44,536
33		15	(h)	Aston Villa	L	2-4	Iversen, Armstrong	35,304
34		19	(a)	Leicester City	W	1-0	Ginola	19,764
35		22	(h)	Wimbledon	W	2-0	Armstrong, Anderton	33,089
36		29	(h)	Derby County	D	1-1	Clemence	33,061
37	May	6	(a)	Manchester United	L	1-3	Armstrong	61,629
38		14	(h)	Sunderland	W	3-1	Anderton (pen), Sherwood, Carr	36,083

FINAL LEAGUE POSITION: 10th in the F.A. Premiership

Appearances

Sub. Appearances

Goals

Appearances grid (shirt number worn per match; * = substituted, † = substitute appearance, ° = sent off / other mark):

Walker IM	Carr S	Edinburgh JC	Freund S	Perry CJ	Campbell SJ	Anderton DR	Sherwood TA	Iversen S	Dominguez JMM	Ginola DDM	Scales JR	Ferdinand L	Leonhardsen O	Taricco MR	Young LP	Nielsen A	Armstrong CP	Vega R	King LB	Piercy JW	Fox RA	Clemence SN	Korsten W	Davies S	Etherington M	McEwan D	Doherty G	No.
1	2	3	4	5	6*	7	8	9	10†	11°	12	13	14															1
1	2		14	5		7	4	9	13†	11	6	10*	8	3°	12													2
1	2		12	5		7*	4	9		11	6	10	8	3														3
1	2		12	5		7	4	9		11*		10	8	3	6													4
1	2		4	5			8	9	12†	11		10*	7	3	6	13												5
1	2		4	5			8	9		11*		10†	7	3	6	13	12											6
1	2		4	5			8	10	13	11*			7	3	6	12	9†											7
1	2		4	5			8	10	12				7	3	6	11	9*											8
1	2		4	5			8	10		11*			7	3	6†	13	9	12										9
1	2			5	6		14	10		11*			7	3	4†		9°	12	8	13								10
1	2		4		6		8	9		11		10		3	5*		12			13	7†							11
1	2		4	12	6		13	9	14	11†		10°		3	5					7*		8						12
1	2	3		5	6		8	10	13	11*			7†				9				12	4						13
1	3	4		5	6		8	10	12	11*			7	2			9											14
1	3	4†		5	6		8	10	13	11			7	2			9*					12						15
1		4	5	6			8†	9	10*	11			7	3	2	12	13											16
1	14	4†	5	6			12	10		11*			7	2	8	9°	3					13						17
1	2		5	6			8	10	12	11*			3		4	9					7							18
1	2		5	6			8	10		11			3	12	4*	9					7							19
1	2		5	6			8	10		11			3	4	9						7							20
1	2	3	5	6	7	8	10	11							9						4							21
1	2	3*	5	6	7	8	10	11†						12	13	9					4							22
1	2	3*	5	6	7	8	10	11						12	13	9°					4†	14						23
1	2		5	6	7*	8	10†	11				3		12	9						4	13						24
1	2		5	6	7	8	13	11*				3		12	9						4†	10						25
1	2	4	5	6	7	8†		11		10	3*	12		9							13							26
1	2	4	5	6	7	10		11		13	8*	3†	12	9														27
1	2	4	5*	6	7	10		11		8	3	12		9														28
1	2	4	5	6*	7	10†		11°		13	8	3	12	9									14					29
1	2	4	5		7	10*		11	6	13	8†	3		9							12							30
1	2	4	5	6	7	10		11			3			9							12	8*						31
1	2	4	5	6	7	10		11†			3			9							8*	12	13					32
1	2	4	5	6	7	10		11			3			9							8							33
1	2	4	5	6	7	10°		11		3*	12			9†							8	13		14				34
1	2	4	5	6	7	10		11*						9							3	8		12				35
1	2		5	6	7	10°		11†		3				9							4	8*	12	14	13			36
1	2	4	5	6	7	10†							9°	14							3	13	8	11*	12			37
1	2	4	5	6	7	12	10†	11				8*		9	3									13				38
38	**34**	**7**	**24**	**36**	**29**	**22**	**23**	**36**	**2**	**36**	**3**	**5**	**21**	**29**	**11**	**5**	**29**	**2**	**2**	**1**	**1**	**16**	**4**	**1**	**1**			
	1	3	1			4			10		1	4	1	9	9	2	3	1	2	2	2	4	5	2	4	1	2	
	3		1			3	8	14		3		2	4				14	1				1						

77

2000-2001

1	Aug	19	(h)	Ipswich Town	W	3-1	Anderton (pen), Carr, Ferdinand	36,044
2		22	(a)	Middlesbrough	D	1-1	Leonhardsen	31,254
3		26	(a)	Newcastle United	L	0-2		51,503
4	Sep	5	(h)	Everton	W	3-2	Rebrov 2 (1 pen), Ferdinand	35,923
5		11	(h)	West Ham United	W	1-0	Campbell	33,133
6		16	(a)	Charlton Athletic	L	0-1		20,043
7		23	(h)	Manchester City	D	0-0		36,065
8		30	(a)	Leeds United	L	3-4	Revrov 2, Perry	37,562
9	Oct	14	(a)	Coventry City	L	1-2	Rebrov	21,430
10		21	(h)	Derby County	W	3-1	Leonhardsen 2, Carr	34,459
11		28	(a)	Chelsea	L	0-3		34,934
12	Nov	4	(h)	Sunderland	W	2-1	Sherwood, Armstrong	36,079
13		11	(a)	Aston Villa	L	0-2		33,608
14		19	(h)	Liverpool	W	2-1	Ferdinand, Sherwood	36,051
15		25	(h)	Leicester City	W	3-0	Ferdinand 3	35,638
16	Dec	2	(a)	Manchester United	L	0-2		67,583
17		9	(a)	Bradford City	D	3-3	King, Campbell, Armstrong	17,225
18		18	(h)	Arsenal	D	1-1	Rebrov	36,062
19		23	(h)	Middlesbrough	D	0-0		35,638
20		27	(a)	Southampton	L	0-2		15,237
21		30	(a)	Ipswich Town	L	0-3		22,234
22	Jan	2	(h)	Newcastle United	W	4-2	Doherty, Armstrong (pen), Rebrov, Ferdinand	34,323
23		13	(a)	Everton	D	0-0		32,290
24		20	(h)	Southampton	D	0-0		36,091
25		31	(a)	West Ham United	D	0-0		26,048
26	Feb	3	(h)	Charlton Athletic	D	0-0		35,368
27		10	(a)	Manchester City	W	1-0	Rebrov	34,399
28		24	(h)	Leeds United	L	1-2	Ferdinand	36,070
29	Mar	3	(a)	Derby County	L	1-2	West (og)	29,410
30		17	(h)	Coventry City	W	3-0	Iversen, Ferdinand, Rebrov	35,606
31		31	(a)	Arsenal	L	0-2		38,121
32	Apr	10	(h)	Bradford City	W	2-1	Iversen, Davies	28,300
33		14	(a)	Sunderland	W	3-2	Clemence, Doherty 2	45,826
34		17	(h)	Chelsea	L	0-3		36,079
35		22	(a)	Liverpool	L	1-3	Korsten	43,547
36		28	(h)	Aston Villa	D	0-0		36,096
37	May	5	(a)	Leicester City	L	2-4	Davies, Carr	21,056
38		19	(h)	Manchester United	W	3-1	Korsten 2, Ferdinand	36,078

FINAL LEAGUE POSITION: 12th in the F.A. Premiership

Appearances

Sub. Appearances

Goals

Sullivan N	Carr S	Thatcher BD	Freund S	Perry CJ	Campbell SJ	Anderton DR	Sherwood TA	Rebrov S	Iversen S	Leonhardsen O	Taricco MR	Ferdinand L	Young LP	Clemence SN	Vega R	Doherty GMT	Walker IM	Dominguez JMM	Davies S	Korsten W	Armstrong CP	Thelwell AA	King LB	McEwan D	Booth AD	Etherington M	Gardner A	Piercy JW	
1	2	3*	4	5	6	7	8	9	10†	11	12	13																	1
1	2	3	4	5	6	7	8	9*	10	11	12																		2
1	2	3†	4	5	6	7	8	9	10*	11°	12	13	14																3
1	2	3*	4	5	6	7°	8	9	14	11	12	10†		13															4
1	2	12	4		6		8	9	7	11	3*	10	5†		13														5
1	2		4	12	6		8*	9	7	11†	3	10		13	5														6
1	2	3*	4	5			8	9	7	11		10†	13		6	12													7
1	2	3	4	5		12	8	9	7	11		10*			6														8
	2	3	4*	5		7	8	9	12	11†		10			6		1	13											9
1	2	3		5		7°	8	9†		11*		10			4	6		14	12	13									10
1	2	4*	5			7	8					9	3	11	6	12			13	10†									11
1	2	3	5			7	8	9*				10	4	11	6				12										12
1	2	3	5			7	8	9*				10†	4	11	6	12			13										13
1	2	12	5			7	8*	9†				10	4	3					13		6	11							14
1	2†	13	12	5*	6	7	8	9°				10							14		4	11							15
1	2		5	6		7	8					10		3					12	9*	4	11							16
1	2	7	5	6			8*					10		3		12			13	9†	4	11							17
1	2		5	6		7	8	9*				10							12		4	11							18
1	2		5	6		7	8*	9		12		10†							13		4	11							19
1	2*		5	6		7	12	9°		8				3		13		14		10†	4	11							20
1			5	6		7	8†		13		2			3		9		12		10*	4	11							21
1			5	6		7†	8	9		2*		10		13	3			12			4	11							22
1			5			7	8	9		2*	4			3	6				12	10†		11	13						23
			8*	5	6	7	9	12	10†	2	3	4					1					11	13						24
			8	5	6	7	9†	2	12		3*	4					1					11	13	10					25
1			8	5	6	7	13	9		2	3†	4										11*	10		12				26
1	13	8	5†	6		7*	11	9		2	3	10									4				12				27
1			8		6		11	9	12	10°	2	3*			5	7†					13		4			14			28
1			8		6	7	12	10		2	3*				5						4†	11		9		13			29
1			8	5	6		9	7		2	3	10									4	11							30
1			8	5			9			2	3	4							11*	10†		7				13	6	12	31
1	2		5				8	9				10†	7*	4	3	6			11	12	13								32
1	2		5				8	9	7*	6	3	10							11°		4†	13				12		14	33
1	2		5†				8	9		6	3*	10							11°	7	4					12	13	14	34
1	2		8				7			5	3	9							11*	10	4					6		12	35
1	2		8				7	9*		5	3	4							11†	10			13			12	6		36
1	2		8				7	9		5	3	10							11		4					6			37
1	2		12				7	9		5	3	4		8					10							11†	6*	13	38
35	27	10	19	30	21	22	31	28	10	23	2	25	19	27	8	18	3	9	8	3	13	18	3	1	5				
	1	2	2	2		1	2	1	4	2	3	3	4	2	2	4	1	2	4	6	6	3	3	1	5	3	5		
	3			1	2	2	2	9	2	3		10		1		3			2	3	2		1						

2001-2002

#	Month	Date		Opponent	Res	Score	Scorers	Attendance
1	Aug	18	(h)	Aston Villa	D	0-0		36,059
2		20	(a)	Everton	D	1-1	Anderton	29,503
3		25	(a)	Blackburn Rovers	L	1-2	Ziege	24,992
4	Sep	9	(h)	Southampton	W	2-0	Ziege, Davies	33,668
5		16	(h)	Chelsea	L	2-3	Sheringham 2	36,037
6		19	(a)	Sunderland	W	2-1	Ziege, Sheringham	47,310
7		22	(a)	Liverpool	L	0-1		44,116
8		29	(h)	Manchester United	L	3-5	Richards, Ferdinand, Ziege	36,038
9	Oct	15	(h)	Derby County	W	3-1	Ferdinand, Ziege, Poyet	30,148
10		21	(a)	Newcastle United	W	2-0	Speed (og), Poyet	50,593
11		27	(h)	Middlesbrough	W	2-1	Sheringham (pen), Ferdinand	36,062
12	Nov	4	(a)	Leeds United	L	1-2	Poyet	40,203
13		17	(h)	Arsenal	D	1-1	Poyet	36,049
14		24	(a)	West Ham United	W	1-0	Ferdinand	32,780
15	Dec	3	(h)	Bolton Wanderers	W	3-2	Poyet, Ferdinand, Sheringham	32,971
16		8	(a)	Charlton Athletic	L	1-3	Poyet	25,125
17		15	(h)	Fulham	W	4-0	Ferdinand, Anderton, Davies, Rebrov	36,054
18		22	(h)	Ipswich Town	L	1-2	Davies	36,040
19		26	(a)	Southampton	L	0-1		31,719
20		29	(a)	Aston Villa	D	1-1	Ferdinand	41,134
21	Jan	1	(h)	Blackburn Rovers	W	1-0	Richards	35,131
22		12	(a)	Ipswich Town	L	1-2	Poyet	25,077
23		19	(h)	Everton	D	1-1	Ferdinand	36,056
24		30	(h)	Newcastle United	L	1-3	Iversen	35,798
25	Feb	2	(a)	Derby County	L	0-1		27,721
26		9	(h)	Leicester City	W	2-1	Anderton, Davies	35,973
27	Mar	2	(h)	Sunderland	W	2-1	Poyet, Ferdinand	36,062
28		6	(a)	Manchester United	L	0-4		67,059
29		13	(a)	Chelsea	L	0-4		39,652
30		18	(h)	Charlton Athletic	L	0-1		29,602
31		24	(a)	Fulham	W	2-0	Sheringham, Poyet	15,885
32		30	(a)	Middlesbrough	D	1-1	Iversen	31,258
33	Apr	1	(h)	Leeds United	W	2-1	Iversen, Sheringham	35,167
34		6	(a)	Arsenal	L	1-2	Sheringham (pen)	38,186
35		13	(h)	West Ham United	D	1-1	Sheringham	36,083
36		20	(a)	Bolton Wanderers	D	1-1	Iversen	25,817
37		27	(h)	Liverpool	W	1-0	Poyet	36,017
38	May	11	(a)	Leicester City	L	1-2	Sheringham (pen)	21,716

FINAL LEAGUE POSITION: 9th in the F.A. Premiership

Appearances

Sub. Appearances

Goals

Sullivan N	Taricco MR	Ziege C	King LB	Doherty GMT	Bunjevcevic GP	Freund S	Poyet GA	Rebrov S	Ferdinand L	Clemence SN	Perry CJ	Anderton DR	Iversen S	Sheringham EP	Davies S	Leonhardsen O	Thelwell A	Richards DI	Sherwood TA	Thatcher BD	Gardner A	Keller KC	Etherington M	
1	2*	3	4	5	6	7†	8	9	10°	11	12	13	14											1
1	2	3	4	5	6	7*	8			12		11	9	10										2
1	2†	3	4		6	14	8	12	11*		5	7°	9	10	13									3
1	2	3	4	5	6		8	9			7*	10		11	12									4
1	2	3	4		6†	8*		13	9	5		7		10	11	12								5
1	2	3	6		4	8		13	9*	5		7†		10	11	12								6
1	2	3	6		4	8		12	9	5		7		10	11*									7
1	2	3	4			7	8	12	9		5	11*		10	6									8
1	2	3	4			7	8	12	9*		5	11		10	6									9
1	2†	3	4			7	8	13	9*		5	11°		10	12	6		14						10
1	2*	3	4			7	8		9		5	11		10	6			12						11
1	2	3	4			7*	8†	12	9		5	11		10	13	6								12
1	2	3	4			7†	8	13	9*		5	11		10	12	6								13
1		3	4			7	8*		9		5	11		10	2	12		6						14
1		3	4		12	7†	8	9°		13	5*	11		10	2	14		6						15
1		3	4			7*	8		9		5	11	13	10	2†	6		12						16
1		3	4			7	8	12	9*		5	11		10	2	6								17
1	2	3	4				8	14	9†	13	5°	7		10	11*	6		12						18
1	2	3	4			7°	8*	14	9			11		10	12	6		13	5†					19
	2	3†	4			7	8	13	9*		5	11		10				6	12			1		20
	2	3	4			7	8*		9		5	11		10				6	12			1		21
1	2°	3†	4				8	9	10*		5	11	14		13			6	7		12			22
1		3*			12			9†		5		11	14	10	2	7°		6	8		4		13	23
1		3	4				8†	14		5		11	9	10*	2°	13		6	7		12			24
1		3°	4				8	14		5	12		9	10	2†	11		6	7*				13	25
1		3	4					13	9*			7		10	2	12		6	8	5†			11	26
1	2†	3	4				8	13	9*					10		11		6	7	5			12	27
1	2	3°	4				8*		9†			14	13	10		11		6	7	5			12	28
1	2	3	4				8	14	9*			13		10	11			6†	7	5°			12	29
1		3	4				8		9†		5	11	13	10*	2			7	6				12	30
1	11	2					8				5	7*	9	10		12			4	3	6			31
	2						8	9*			5	7†	10		13	12		6	4	3		1	11	32
	2		12	13	14						5	7*	9	10°	2			6	8	3	4	1	11†	33
		3°	2†				8	14			5	11	9*	10		12		6	7		4	1	13	34
		3*		12			8	9†			5	11	13	10	2	7		6			4	1		35
		3		13			8	12†			5	11	9*	10	2	7		6			4	1		36
		3					8		11		5	7	9	10	2			6			4	1		37
		3		13			8		11*		5	7	9	10	2†			6			4	1	12	38
29	30	27	32	4	5	19	32	9	22	4	30	33	12	33	22	2		24	15	11	11	9	3	
	5							3	1	1	2	21	3	2	3	2	6	1	9	5	2	4	1	4	8	
		5					10	1	9			3	4	10	4			2						

2002-2003

1	Aug	17	(a)	Everton	D	2-2	Etherington, Ferdinand	40,120
2		24	(h)	Aston Villa	W	1-0	Redknapp	35,384
3		27	(a)	Charlton Athletic	W	1-0	Davies	26,461
4		31	(h)	Southampton	W	2-1	Ferdinand, Sheringham (pen)	35,573
5	Sep	11	(a)	Fulham	L	2-3	Richards, Sheringham	16,757
6		15	(h)	West Ham United	W	3-2	Davies, Sheringham (pen), Gardner	36,005
7		21	(a)	Manchester United	L	0-1		67,611
8		28	(h)	Middlesbrough	L	0-3		36,082
9	Oct	6	(a)	Blackburn Rovers	W	2-1	Keane, Redknapp	26,203
10		20	(h)	Bolton Wanderers	W	3-1	Keane 2, Davies	35,909
11		26	(a)	Liverpool	L	1-2	Richards	44,084
12	Nov	3	(h)	Chelsea	D	0-0		36,049
13		10	(a)	Sunderland	L	0-2		40,024
14		16	(a)	Arsenal	L	0-3		38,152
15		24	(h)	Leeds United	W	2-0	Sheringham, Keane	35,718
16		30	(a)	Birmingham City	D	1-1	Sheringham	29,505
17	Dec	8	(h)	West Bromwich Alb	W	3-1	Ziege, Keane, Poyet	35,958
18		15	(h)	Arsenal	D	1-1	Ziege	36,076
19		23	(a)	Manchester City	W	3-2	Perry, Davies, Poyet	34,563
20		26	(h)	Charlton Athletic	D	2-2	Keane, Iversen	36,043
21		29	(a)	Newcastle United	L	1-2	Dabizas (og)	52,145
22	Jan	1	(a)	Southampton	L	0-1		31,890
23		12	(h)	Everton	W	4-3	Poyet, Keane 3	36,070
24		18	(a)	Aston Villa	W	1-0	Sheringham	38,576
25		29	(h)	Newcastle United	L	0-1		36,084
26	Feb	1	(h)	Chelsea	D	1-1	Sheringham	41,384
27		8	(a)	Sunderland	W	4-1	Poyet, Doherty, Davies, Sheringham	36,075
28		24	(h)	Fulham	D	1-1	Sheringham	34,704
29	Mar	1	(a)	West Ham United	L	0-2		35,049
30		16	(h)	Liverpool	L	2-3	Taricco, Sheringham	36,077
31		24	(a)	Bolton Wanderers	L	0-1		23,084
32	Apr	5	(h)	Birmingham City	W	2-1	Keane, Poyet	36,058
33		12	(a)	Leeds United	D	2-2	Sheringham, Keane	39,560
34		18	(h)	Manchester City	L	0-2		36,075
35		21	(a)	West Bromwich Alb	W	3-2	Keane 2, Sheringham	26,899
36		27	(h)	Manchester United	L	0-2		36,073
37	May	3	(a)	Middlesbrough	L	1-5	Redknapp	30,230
38		11	(h)	Blackburn Rovers	L	0-4		36,036

FINAL LEAGUE POSITION: 10th in the F.A. Premiership

Appearances

Sub. Appearances

Goals

Keller KC	Carr S	Taricco MR	Bunjevcevic GP	Gardner A	Richards DI	Davies S	Redknapp JF	Iversen S	Sheringham EP	Etherington M	Thatcher BD	Acimovic M	Ferdinand L	Ziege C	Doherty GMT	Blondel J	Perry CJ	Keane RD	Freund S	Poyet GA	Anderton DR	King LB	Slabber J	Toda K	
1	2*	3	4	5	6	7	8	9†	10°	11	12	13	14												1
1		2	14	5	6	7	8		10	11*	12	4	9°	3†	13										2
1		2	4	5	6	7	8		10	11			12	3	9*										3
1	2*	12			6	7	8	14	10	11	3	4°	9†		5	13									4
1		2		5	6	7		14	10	11*	3	8†	9	13	12	4°									5
1	2†	4		5		7	8	14	10	11*	12			3	13	6°	9								6
1		4			6	2	8	7*	10†	11	3	13	12		5		9								7
1		4			6	2	8	7†	14	11	5	13	9*	3°	12		10								8
1	3†	4			6	2	8	13	10		5	11*				12	9	7							9
1	2	3			6	7	8		10	11*							5	9	4	12					10
1	2	3			6	7	8*	10°	12			14	13				5	9	4	11†					11
1	2	3			6	7	8	10†				13	12				5	9	4	11*					12
1	2	14			6	7		12	10		3†	13					5	9	4°	8*	11				13
1	2	3			6	7	8*	13	10°	11†								9	4	14	12	5			14
1	2	4		6	12	14	13	10						3°				9	7	8†	11*	5			15
1	2	4		6		14	13	10			12			3				9†	7	8°	11*	5			16
1	2			6	7	8	12	10†						3			5	9		13	11	4*			17
1	2	4		6	12			10						3				9	7	8	11*	5			18
1	2			6	7	9*								3			5	10	8	12	11	4			19
1	2	6			14	12	10°					13	3				5	9	7†	8	11*	4			20
1	2	3	6			7	9°	14				13	12				5	10†	8	11*		4			21
1	2	3°	8*		6	11†			10			14					5	9	7	13	12	4			22
1	2	3			7	9*			12						6		5	10		8	11	4			23
1	2	3	4		6	7			10									9	12	8*	11	5			24
1	2	3	5		6	7			10							12	9*			8	11	4			25
1	2	3	6	5†		7	9*		10	13						12				8	11	4			26
1	2	3	4*		6	7			10	13					14		9°		12	8†	11	5			27
1	2	3	4		6	7			10	13	12†				9					8*	11	5			28
1	2	3	4*		6	7			10	11†	12	14			9°				13		8	5			29
1	2	3*	4			7			10	11	6				9†				12	8		5	13		30
1	2	3	4			7			10	13	6†				12		9			8	11*	5			31
1	2	3*	6			7			10	12							5	9		8	11	4			32
1	2	3	6	5		7			10	12							9			8*	11	4			33
1	2	3†	6°	5		7			10			14				12	9			8*	11	4	13		34
1	2		3	5	6†	7			10	11						12	9			13	4	8*			35
1	2	3	13	12	6*	7		14	10	11°							9			4	5	8†			36
1	2	3	8	6		7	13		10†	12							5	9		11*	4				37
1	2	3*				7	4†		10	11					12		5	9		8	6	13			38
38	30	21	31	11	26	33	14	8	34	15	8	4	4	10	7	15	29	13	22	18	25	2			
	4	1		3	3	11	2	8	4	13	7	2	8	1	3		4	6	2		1	2			
		1		1	2	5	3	1	12	1			2	2	1		1	13		5					

2003-2004

#	Month	Date		Opponent	Res	Score	Scorers	Attendance
1	Aug	16	(a)	Birmingham City	L	0-1		29,358
2		23	(h)	Leeds United	W	2-1	Taricco, Kanoute	34,354
3		27	(a)	Liverpool	D	0-0		43,778
4		30	(h)	Fulham	L	0-3		33,421
5	Sep	13	(a)	Chelsea	L	2-4	Kanoute 2	41,165
6		20	(h)	Southampton	L	1-3	Kanoute	35,784
7		28	(a)	Manchester City	D	0-0		46,842
8	Oct	4	(h)	Everton	W	3-0	Kanoute, Poyet, Keane	36,137
9		19	(a)	Leicester City	W	2-1	Mabizela, Kanoute	31,521
10		26	(h)	Middlesbrough	D	0-0		32,643
11	Nov	1	(h)	Bolton Wanderers	L	0-1		35,191
12		8	(a)	Arsenal	L	1-2	Anderton	38,101
13		23	(h)	Aston Villa	W	2-1	Ricketts, Keane	33,140
14		29	(a)	Blackburn Rovers	L	0-1		22,802
15	Dec	6	(h)	Wolves	W	5-2	Keane 3, Kanoute, Dalmat	34,825
16		13	(a)	Newcastle United	L	0-4		52,139
17		21	(h)	Manchester United	L	1-2	Poyet	35,910
18		26	(a)	Portsmouth	L	0-2		20,078
19		28	(h)	Charlton Athletic	L	0-1		34,534
20	Jan	7	(h)	Birmingham City	W	4-1	Dalmat 2, Davies, Keane	30,016
21		10	(a)	Leeds United	W	1-0	Keane	35,365
22		17	(h)	Liverpool	W	2-1	Keane (pen), Postiga	36,104
23		31	(a)	Fulham	L	1-2	Keane (pen)	17,024
24	Feb	7	(h)	Portsmouth	W	4-3	Defoe, Keane 2, Poyet	36,107
25		11	(a)	Charlton Athletic	W	4-2	Davies, Defoe, King, Jackson	26,660
26		22	(h)	Leicester City	D	4-4	Brown, Defoe 2, Keane	35,218
27	Mar	9	(a)	Middlesbrough	L	0-1		31,789
28		14	(h)	Newcastle United	W	1-0	O'Brien (og)	36,083
29		20	(a)	Manchester United	L	0-3		67,634
30		27	(a)	Southampton	L	0-1		31,973
31	Apr	3	(h)	Chelsea	L	0-1		36,101
32		9	(a)	Everton	L	1-3	Carr	38,086
33		12	(h)	Manchester City	D	1-1	Defoe	35,282
34		17	(a)	Bolton Wanderers	L	0-2		26,440
35		25	(h)	Arsenal	D	2-2	Redknapp, Keane	36,097
36	May	2	(a)	Aston Villa	L	0-1		42,573
37		8	(h)	Blackburn Rovers	W	1-0	Defoe	35,698
38		15	(a)	Wolves	W	2-0	Keane, Defoe	29,389

FINAL LEAGUE POSITION: 14th in the F.A. Premiership

Appearances

Sub. Appearances

Goals

Keller KC	Carr S	Taricco MR	Bunjevcevic GP	Gardner A	Doherty GMT	Davies S	Redknapp JF	Postiga H	Keane RD	Ricketts RA	Marney D	Zamora RL	King LB	Kanoute F	Richards DI	Anderton DR	Konchesky PM	Dalmat S	Poyet GA	Mabizela M	Blondel J	Jackson J	Kelly S	Brown M	Ziege C	Defoe JC	Yeates M	
1	2	3*	4	5	6	7	8	9†	10	11	12	13																1
1	2	3*		5		7	8	9		11	12	10†	4	13	6													2
1	2	3		5		7	8	9*		11		10†	4	13	6	12												3
1	2	3		5		7*	8	9		11		13	4†	10	6	12												4
1	2	3*	13	5			8			11		10	4†	9	6		7°	12	14									5
1	2	3	4*	5			8			12	14	11	10°	9	6	13		7†										6
1	2	3	4*	5					10	12			9		6	7	11†	13	8									7
1	2	3*		5				13	10	11			9†		6	7	4	12	8									8
1	2	3		5					10	11°		12		9	6	7	4*	14	8†	13								9
1	2	3	5					14	10	12			9°	13	6	7	4*	11	8†									10
1	2	3*		5				14	10				9	4†	6	7	11		8°	13	12							11
1	2	3	5					9†	10	12			13	4	6	7	11°	8*		14								12
1	2	3	5					9*	10	13			12	4	6	7	11†	8										13
1	2	3	5					9†	10	14			13	4	6	7	11°	8*		12								14
1	2	3	5						10	11†			4	9	6	7	13	12	8*									15
1	2	3	5					13	10				4	9†	6	7	11°	14	8*	12								16
1	2	3*	5					14	10	12			4	9	6	7†	11	8°	13									17
1	2	3	5					12	10	14			13	4	9†	6		11°	8*	7								18
1		3*	5					13	10	11°			14	4	9	6		8†	12	7	2							19
1	2			6	7			13	10	12			5	9†		11°		8*	4		3	14						20
1	2	3	5	6	7				10				4	9		11*		8	12									21
1	2	3	5	6	7			9†	10			13		11				8*				12		4				22
1	2		5		7			9*	10			12	4					11						8	3			23
1	2		5		7				10	13			4		6			11†	12			3		8		9*		24
1	2	3		5	7				10				4		6				12			11		8		9*		25
1	2	3		5	7				10				4	12	6	13						11†		8*		9		26
1	2	3	5					12	10				4		6	7*		14	13			11°		8†		9		27
1	2	3	5	6		12			10				4	7*				13						8	11†	9		28
1	2	3*	5	6		13			10			7†	4	14				12						8	11	9°		29
1	2		5	6		14			10				4	7				13				11°	12	8†	3*	9		30
1	2	3*	5	6		7†			10				4	14								13	12	8	11°	9		31
1	2	12	5	6	7†	4*			10	13			14									3	8	11°	9			32
1	2*	3†	13	5	6	7	4		14					9			11°					12	8		10			33
1	14		5	6	7†	4*		12	13				3	9			11°					2	8		10			34
1	3	13	5		7	4		10					6	9			12			11°	2*	8			14			35
1	3		5	13	7	4		11	12				9†	6							2*	8			10			36
1	3*		5		7	4†		10	11°				6	14			13				2	8	12	9				37
1			5			4		10*	11†				6	13			12				2	8	3	9	7			38
38	32	31	3	33	16	17	14	9	31	12	1	6	28	19	23	16	10	12	12			9	7	17	7	14	1	
	1	4		1		3	10	3	12	2	10	1	8		4	2	10	8	6	1	2	4		1	1			
	1	1			2	1	1	14	1		1	7			1	3	3	1		1		1		7				

F.A. CUP

1974/75 SEASON
3rd Round
Jan 4 vs Nottingham Forest (a) 1-1
Att: 23,355   Chivers

Replay
Jan 8 vs Nottingham Forest (h) 0-1
Att: 27,996

1975/76 SEASON
3rd Round
Jan 3 vs Stoke City (h) 1-1
Att: 26,715   Duncan

Replay
Jan 24 vs Stoke City (a) 1-2
Att: 29,751   Perryman

1976/77 SEASON
3rd Round
Jan 8 vs Cardiff City (a) 0-1
Att: 27,868

1977/78 SEASON
3rd Round
Jan 7 vs Bolton Wanderers (h) 2-2
Att: 43,731   Hoddle, Duncan

Replay
Jan 10 vs Bolton Wanderers (a) 1-2 (aet.)
Att: 31,314   Taylor (pen)

1978/79 SEASON
3rd Round
Jan 10 vs Altrincham (h) 1-1
Att: 31,081   Taylor (pen)

Replay (at Maine Road)
Jan 16 vs Altrincham (h) 3-0
Att: 27,878   Lee 3

4th Round
Feb 12 vs Wrexham (h) 3-3
Att: 27,120   Hoddle, Jones, Roberts (og)

Replay
Feb 21 vs Wrexham (a) 3-2 (aet.)
Att: 16,050   Jones 3

5th Round
Feb 28 vs Oldham Athletic (a) 1-0
Att: 16,097   Perryman

6th Round
Mar 10 vs Manchester United (h) 1-1
Att: 51,800   Ardiles

Replay
Mar 14 vs Manchester United (a) 0-2
Att: 54,510

1979/80 SEASON
3rd Round
Jan 5 vs Manchester United (h) 1-1
Att: 45,207   Ardiles

Replay
Jan 9 vs Manchester United (a) 1-0 (aet.)
Att: 53,762   Ardiles

4th Round
Jan 26 vs Swindon Town (a) 0-0
Att: 26,000

Replay
Jan 30 vs Swindon Town (h) 2-1
Att: 46,707   Armstrong 2

5th Round
Feb 16 vs Birmingham City (h) 3-1
Att: 49,936   Armstrong, Hoddle 2 (1 pen)

6th Round
Mar 8 vs Liverpool (h) 0-1
Att: 48,033

1980/81 SEASON
3rd Round
Jan 3 vs Queen's Park Rangers (a) 0-0
Att: 28,829

Replay
Jan 7 vs Queen's Park Rangers (h) 3-1
Att: 36,294   Galvin, Hoddle, Crooks

4th Round
Jan 24 vs Hull City (h) 2-0
Att: 37,532   Archibald, Brooke

5th Round
Feb 14 vs Coventry City (h) 3-1
Att: 36,688   Hughton, Ardiles, Archibald

6th Round
March 7 vs Exeter City (h) 2-0
Att: 40,629   Miller, Roberts

Semi-Final (at Hillsborough)
Apr 11 vs Wolverhampton Wanderers 2-2
Att: 40,174   Archibald, Hoddle

Replay (at Highbury)
Apr 15 vs Wolverhampton Wanderers 3-0
Att: 52,539   Villa, Crooks 2

FINAL (at Wembley)
May 9 vs Manchester City 1-1 (aet.)
Att: 100,000   Hutchinson (og)

Replay (at Wembley)
May 14 vs Manchester City 3-2
Att: 96,000   Villa 2, Crooks

1981/82 SEASON
3rd Round
Jan 2 vs Arsenal (h) 1-0
Att: 38,421   Crooks

4th Round
Jan 23 vs Leeds United (h) 1-0
Att: 46,126   Crooks

5th Round
Feb 13 vs Aston Villa (h) 1-0
Att: 43,419   Falco

6th Round
Mar 6 vs Chelsea (a) 3-2
Att: 42,557   Hoddle, Archibald, Hoddle

Semi-Final (at Villa Park)
Apr 3 vs Leicester City 2-0
Att: 46,606   Crooks, Wilson (og)

FINAL (at Wembley)
May 22 vs Queen's Park Rangers 1-1 (aet.)
Att: 100,000   Hoddle

Replay (at Wembley)
May 27 vs Queen's Park Rangers 1-0
Att: 92,000   Hoddle (pen)

1982/83 SEASON
3rd Round
Jan 8 vs Southampton (h) 1-0
Att: 38,040   Hazard

4th Round
Jan 29 vs West Bromwich Albion (h) 2-1
Att: 38,208   Gibson, Crooks

5th Round
Feb 19 vs Everton (a) 0-2
Att: 42,995

1983/84 SEASON
3rd Round
Jan 7 vs Fulham (a) 0-0
Att: 23,398

Replay
Jan 11 vs Fulham (h) 2-0
Att: 32,898   Roberts, Archibald

4th Round
Jan 28 vs Norwich City (h) 0-0
Att: 37,792

Replay
Feb 1 vs Norwich City (a) 1-2
Att: 26,811   Falco

1984/85 SEASON
3rd Round
Jan 5 vs Charlton Athletic (h) 1-1
Att: 29,029   Crooks

Replay
Jan 23 vs Charlton Athletic (a) 2-1
Att: 21,409   Falco, Galvin

4th Round
Jan 27 vs Liverpool (a) 0-1
Att: 27,905

1985/86 SEASON
3rd Round
Jan 4 vs Oxford United (a) 1-1
Att: 10,638   Chiedozie

Replay
Jan 8 vs Oxford United (h) 2-1 (aet.)
Att: 19,136   Waddle, C. Allen

4th Round
Jan 25 vs Notts County (a) 1-1
Att: 17,546   C. Allen

Replay
Jan 29 vs Notts County (h) 5-0
Att: 17,393   Chiedozie, Falco, C. Allen, Hoddle, Waddle

5th Round
Mar 4 vs Everton (h) 1-2
Att: 23,338   Falco

1986/87 SEASON
3rd Round
Jan 10 vs Scunthorpe United (h) 3-2
Att: 19,339   Mabbutt, Waddle, Claesen

4th Round
Jan 31 vs Crystal Palace (h) 4-0
Att: 29,603   Mabbutt, C. Allen (pen), Claesen, O'Reilly (og)

5th Round
Feb 21 vs Newcastle United (h) 1-0
Att: 38,033   C. Allen (pen)

6th Round
Mar 15 vs Wimbledon (h) 2-0
Att: 15,636   Waddle, Hoddle

Semi-Final (at Villa Park)
Apr 11 vs Watford 4-1
Att: 46,151   Hodge 2, C. Allen, P. Allen

FINAL (at Wembley)
May 16 vs Coventry City 2-3 (aet.)
Att: 98,000   C. Allen, Mabbutt

1987/88 SEASON
3rd Round
Jan 9 vs Oldham Athletic (a) 4-2
Att: 16,931   Thomas, C. Allen 2, Waddle

4th Round
Jan 30 vs Port Vale (a) 1-2
Att: 20,045   Ruddock

1988/89 SEASON
3rd Round
Jan 7 vs Bradford City (a) 0-1
Att: 15,917

1989/90 SEASON
3rd Round
Jan 6 vs Southampton (h) 1-3
Att: 33,134   Howells

1990/91 SEASON
3rd Round
Jan 5 vs Blackpool (a) 1-0
Att: 9,563 Stewart

4th Round
Jan 26 vs Oxford United (h) 4-2
Att: 31,665 Mabbutt, Gascoigne 2, Lineker

5th Round
Feb 16 vs Portsmouth (a) 2-1
Att: 26,049 Gascoigne 2

6th Round
Mar 10 vs Notts County (h) 2-1
Att: 29,686 Nayim, Gascoigne

Semi-Final (at Wembley)
Apr 14 vs Arsenal 3-1
Att: 77,893 Gascoigne, Lineker 2

FINAL (at Wembley)
May 18 vs Nottingham Forest 2-1 (aet.)
Att: 80,000 Stewart, Walker (og)

1991/92 SEASON
3rd Round
Jan 5 vs Aston Villa (a) 0-0
Att: 29,316

Replay
Jan 14 vs Aston Villa (h) 0-1
Att: 25,462

1992/93 SEASON
3rd Round (at White Hart Lane)
Jan 2 vs Marlow (a) 5-1
Att: 26,636 Barmby 2, Samways 2, Sheringham

4th Round
Jan 24 vs Norwich City (a) 2-0
Att: 15,005 Sheringham 2

5th Round
Feb 14 vs Wimbledon (h) 3-2
Att: 26,529 Anderton, Sheringham, Barmby

6th Round
Mar 7 vs Manchester City (a) 4-2
Att: 34,050 Nayim 3, Sedgley

Semi-Final (at Wembley)
Apr 4 vs Arsenal 0-1
Att: 76,263

1993/94 SEASON
3rd Round
Jan 8 vs Peterborough United (a) 1-1
Att: 19,169 Dozzell

Replay
Jan 19 vs Peterborough United (h) 1-1 (aet)
Att: 24,893 Barmby
Tottenham won 5-4 on penalties

4th Round
Jan 29 vs Ipswich Town (a) 0-3
Att: 22,539

1994/95 SEASON
3rd Round
Jan 7 vs Altrincham (h) 3-0
Att: 25,057 Sheringham, Rosenthal, Nethercott

4th Round
Jan 29 vs Sunderland (a) 4-1
Att: 21,135 Klinsmann 2 (1 pen), Sheringham, Melville (og)

5th Round
Feb 18 vs Southampton (h) 1-1
Att: 28,091 Klinsmann

Replay
Mar 1 vs Southampton (a) 6-2 (aet.)
Att: 15,172 Rosenthal 3, Sheringham,

Barmby, Anderton

6th Round
Mar 11 vs Liverpool (a) 2-1
Att: 39,592 Sheringham, Klinsmann

Semi-Final (at Elland Road)
Apr 9 vs Everton (a) 1-4
Att: 38,226 Klinsmann (pen)

1995/96 SEASON
3rd Round
Jan 6 vs Hereford United (a) 1-1
Att: 8,806 Rosenthal

Replay
Jan 17 vs Hereford United (h) 5-1
Att: 31,534 Sheringham 3, Armstrong 2

4th Round
Jan 27 vs Wolverhampton Wands. (h) 1-1
Att: 32,812 Wilson

Replay
Feb 7 vs Wolverhampton Wanderers (a) 2-0
Att: 27,846 Rosenthal, Sheringham

5th Round
Feb 28 vs Nottingham Forest (a) 2-2
Att: 18,600 Armstrong 2

Replay
Mar 9 vs Nottingham Forest (h) 1-1 (aet.)
Att: 31,055 Sheringham
Nottingham Forest won 3-1 on penalties

1996/97 SEASON
3rd Round
Jan 5 vs Manchester United (a) 0-2
Att: 52,495

1997/98 SEASON
3rd Round
Jan 5 vs Fulham (h) 3-1
Att: 27,909 Clemence, Calderwood, Taylor (og)

4th Round
Jan 24 vs Barnsley (h) 1-1
Att: 28,722 Campbell

Replay
Feb 4 vs Barnsley (a) 1-3
Att: 18,220 Ginola

1998/99 SEASON
3rd Round
Jan 2 vs Watford (h) 5-2
Att: 36,022 Iversen 2, Anderton (pen), Nielsen, Fox

4th Round
Jan 23 vs Wimbledon (a) 1-1
Att: 22,229 Ginola

Replay
Feb 2 vs Wimbledon (h) 3-0
Att: 24,049 Sinton, Nielsen 2

5th Round
Feb 13 vs Leeds United (a) 1-1
Att: 36,696 Sherwood

Replay
Feb 24 vs Leeds United (h) 2-0
Att: 32,307 Anderton, Ginola

6th Round
Mar 16 vs Barnsley (a) 1-0
Att: 18,793 Ginola

Semi-Final (at Old Trafford)
Apr 11 vs Newcastle United 0-2
Att: 53,609

1999/2000 SEASON
3rd Round
Dec 12 vs Newcastle United (h) 1-1
Att: 33,116 Iversen

Replay
Dec 22 vs Newcastle Utd. (a) 1-6
Att: 35,415 Ginola

2000/2001 SEASON
3rd Round
Jan 6 vs Leyton Orient (a) 1-0
Att: 12,336 Doherty

4th Round
Feb 7 vs Charlton Athletic (a) 4-2
Att: 18,101 Rufus (og), Anderton, Leonhardsen, Rebrov

5th Round
Feb 17 vs Stockport County (h) 4-0
Att: 36,040 King, Davies 2, Flynn (og)

6th Round
Mar 11 vs West Ham United (a) 3-2
Att: 26,048 Rebrov 2, Doherty

Semi-Final (at Old Trafford)
Apr 8 vs Arsenal 1-2
Att: 63,541 Doherty

2001/2002 SEASON
3rd Round
Jan 16 vs Coventry City (a) 2-0
Att: 20,758 Poyet, Ferdinand

4th Round
Feb 5 vs Bolton Wanderers (h) 4-0
Att: 27,093 Anderton (pen), Iversen, Etherington, Barness (og)

5th Round
Feb 17 vs Tranmere Rovers (h) 4-0
Att: 35,696 Ziege, Poyet 2, Sheringham

6th Round
Mar 10 vs Chelsea (h) 0-4
Att: 32,896

2002/2003 SEASON
3rd Round
Jan 4 vs Southampton (a) 0-4
Att: 25,589

2003/2004 SEASON
3rd Round
Jan 3 vs Crystal Palace (h) 3-0
Att: 32,340 Kanoute 3

4th Round
Jan 25 vs Manchester City (a) 1-1
Att: 28,840 Doherty

Replay
Feb 4 vs Manchester City (h) 3-4
Att: 30,400 King, Keane, Ziege

LEAGUE CUP COMPETITION

1974/75 SEASON
2nd Round
Sep 11 vs Middlesbrough (h) 0-4
Att: 15,216

1975/76 SEASON
2nd Round
Sep 9 vs Watford (a) 1-0
Att: 14,997 Jones

3rd Round
Oct 8 vs Crewe Alexandra (a) 2-0
Att: 10,561 Pratt, Conn

4th Round
Nov 12 vs West Ham United (h) 0-0
Att: 49,161

Replay
Nov 24 vs West Ham United (a) 2-0 (aet.)
Att: 38,443 Young, Duncan

5th Round
Dec 3 vs Doncaster Rovers (h) 7-2
Att: 25,702   Pratt, Chivers 2, Duncan 3, Chappell (og)

Semi-Final (1st leg)
Jan 14 vs Newcastle United (h) 1-0
Att: 40,215   Pratt

Semi-Final (2nd leg)
Jan 21 vs Newcastle Utd. (a) 1-3 (agg. 2-3)
Att: 49,657   McAllister

1976/77 SEASON
2nd Round
Aug 31 vs Middlesbrough (a) 2-1
Att: 19,042   Moores, Neighbour

3rd Round
Sep 22 vs Wrexham (h) 2-3
Att: 19,156   Hoddle, Moores

1977/78 SEASON
2nd Round
Aug 31 vs Wimbledon (h) 4-0
Att: 22,807   Osgood (pen), Duncan 3

3rd Round
Oct 26 vs Coventry City (h) 2-3
Att: 35,099   Pratt, Armstrong

1978/79 SEASON
2nd Round
Aug 29 vs Swansea City (a) 2-2
Att: 24,335   Hoddle (pen), Armstrong

Replay
Sep 6 vs Swansea City (h) 1-3
Att: 33,672   Villa

1979/80 SEASON
2nd Round (1st leg)
Aug 29 vs Manchester United (h) 2-1
Att: 29,163   Pratt, Hoddle

2nd Round (2nd leg)
Sep 5 vs Manchester Utd. (a) 1-3 (agg. 3-4)
Att: 48,292   Armstrong

1980/81 SEASON
2nd Round (1st leg)
Aug 27 vs Orient (a) 1-0
Att: 20,087   Lacy

2nd Round (2nd leg)
Sep 3 vs Orient (h) 3-1 (aggregate 4-1)
Att: 25,806   Archibald 2, Crooks

3rd Round
Sep 24 vs Crystal Palace (h) 0-0
Att: 29,654

Replay
Sep 30 vs Crystal Palace (a) 3-1 (aet.)
Att: 26,885   Villa, Hoddle, Crooks

4th Round
Nov 4 vs Arsenal (h) 1-0
Att: 42,511   Ardiles

5th Round
Dec 2 vs West Ham United (a) 0-1
Att: 36,003

1981/82 SEASON
2nd Round (1st leg)
Oct 7 vs Manchester United (h) 1-0
Att: 39,333   Archibald

2nd Round (2nd leg)
Oct 28 vs Manchester U. (a) 1-0 (agg. 2-0)
Att: 55,890   Hazard

3rd Round
Nov 11 vs Wrexham (h) 2-0
Att: 24,084   Hughton, Hoddle

4th Round
Dec 2 vs Fulham (h) 1-0
Att: 30,214   Hazard

5th Round
Jan 18 vs Nottingham Forest (h) 1-0
Att: 31,192   Ardiles

Semi-Final (1st leg)
Feb 3 vs West Bromwich Albion (a) 0-0
Att: 32,238

Semi-Final (2nd leg)
Feb 10 vs West Brom. A. (h) 1-0 (agg. 1-0)
Att: 47,241   Hazard

FINAL (at Wembley)
Mar 13 vs Liverpool 1-3 (aet.)
Att: 100,000

1982/83 SEASON
2nd Round (1st leg)
Oct 6 vs Brighton & Hove Albion (h) 1-1
Att: 20,416   Brooke (pen)

2nd Round (2nd leg)
Oct 25 vs Brighton & HA (a) 1-0 (agg. 2-1)
Att: 20,755   Crooks

3rd Round
Nov 9 vs Gillingham (a) 4-2
Att: 14,366   Archibald 2, Crooks 2

4th Round
Dec 1 vs Luton Town (h) 1-0
Att: 27,861   Villa

5th Round
Jan 19 vs Burnley (h) 1-4
Att: 30,771   Gibson

1983/84 SEASON
2nd Round (1st leg)
Oct 5 vs Lincoln City (h) 3-1
Att: 20,491   Galvin, Archibald, Houghton (og)

2nd Round (2nd leg)
Oct 26 vs Lincoln City (a) 1-2 (agg. 4-3)
Att: 12,239   Falco

3rd Round
Nov 9 vs Arsenal (h) 1-2
Att: 48,200   Hoddle (pen)

1984/85 SEASON
2nd Round (1st leg)
Sep 26 vs Halifax Town (a) 5-1
Att: 7,027   Falco 2, Crooks 3

2nd Round (2nd leg)
Oct 9 vs Halifax Town (h) 4-0 (agg. 9-1)
Att: 14,802   Hughton, Hazard 2, Crooks

3rd Round
Oct 31 vs Liverpool (h) 1-0
Att: 38,690   Allen

4th Round
Nov 21 vs Sunderland (a) 0-0
Att: 27,421

Replay
Dec 5 vs Sunderland (h) 1-2
Att: 25,835   Roberts (pen)

1985/86 SEASON
2nd Round (1st leg)
Sep 23 vs Orient (a) 0-2
Att: 13,828

2nd Round (2nd leg)
Oct 30 vs Orient (h) 4-0 (aggregate 4-2)
Att: 21,046   Roberts 2, Galvin, Waddle

3rd Round
Nov 6 vs Wimbledon (h) 2-0
Att: 16,899   Leworthy, Mabbutt

4th Round
Nov 20 vs Portsmouth (h) 0-0
Att: 28,619

Replay
Nov 27 vs Portsmouth (a) 0-0 (aet.)
Att: 28,100

2nd Replay
Dec 10 vs Portsmouth (a) 0-1
Att: 26,306

1986/87 SEASON
2nd Round (1st leg)
Sep 23 vs Barnsley (a) 3-2
Att: 10,079   Roberts, C. Allen, Waddle

2nd Round (2nd leg)
Oct 8 vs Barnsley (h) 5-3 (aggregate 8-5)
Att: 12,299   Close, Hoddle 2, Galvin, C. Allen

3rd Round
Oct 29 vs Birmingham City (h) 5-0
Att: 15,542   Roberts, C. Allen 2, Hoddle, Waddle

4th Round
Nov 26 vs Cambridge United (a) 3-1
Att: 10,033   C. Allen, Close, Waddle

5th Round
Jan 27 vs West Ham United (a) 1-1
Att: 28,648   C. Allen

Replay
Feb 2 vs West Ham United (h) 5-0
Att: 41,995   C. Allen 3 (1 pen), Hoddle, Claesen

Semi-Final (1st leg)
Feb 8 vs Arsenal (a) 1-0
Att: 41,256   C. Allen

Semi-Final (2nd leg)
Mar 1 vs Arsenal (h) 1-2 (aet.) (agg. 2-2)
Att: 37,099   C. Allen

Replay
Mar 4 vs Arsenal (h) 1-2
Att: 41,005   C. Allen

1987/88 SEASON
2nd Round (1st leg)
Sep 23 vs Torquay United (a) 0-1
Att: 5,000

2nd Round (2nd leg)
Oct 7 vs Torquay United (h) 3-0 (agg. 3-1)
Att: 20,970   Claesen 2, Croft

3rd Round
Oct 28 vs Aston Villa (a) 1-2
Att: 29,114   Ardiles

1988/89 SEASON
2nd Round (1st leg)
Sep 27 vs Notts County (a) 1-1
Att: 9,269   Samways

2nd Round (2nd leg)
Oct 11 vs Notts County (h) 2-1 (agg. 3-2)
Att: 14,953   Fenwick (pen), Gascoigne

3rd Round
Nov 1 vs Blackburn Rovers (h) 0-0
Att: 18,814

Replay
Nov 9 vs Blackburn Rovers (a) 2-1 (aet.)
Att: 12,961   Thomas, Stewart

4th Round
Nov 29 vs Southampton (a) 1-2
Att: 17,357   Osman (og)

1989/90 SEASON

2nd Round (1st leg)
Sep 20 vs Southend United (h) 1-0
Att: 15,734   Fenwick

2nd Round (2nd leg)
Oct 4 vs Southend U (a) 2-3 (aet.)(agg. 3-3)
Att: 10,400   Allen, Nayim
Tottenham won on the away goals rule

3rd Round
Oct 25 vs Manchester United (a) 3-0
Att: 45,759   Lineker, Samways, Nayim

4th Round
Nov 22 vs Tranmere Rovers (a) 2-2
Att: 13,789   Gascoigne, Higgins (og)

Replay
Nov 29 vs Tranmere Rovers (h) 4-0
Att: 22,720   Allen, Howells, Mabbutt, Stewart

5th Round
Jan 17 vs Nottingham Forest (a) 2-2
Att: 30,044   Lineker, Sedgley

Replay
Jan 24 vs Nottingham Forest (h) 2-3
Att: 32,357   Nayim, Walsh

1990/91 SEASON

2nd Round (1st leg)
Sep 26 vs Hartlepool United (h) 5-0
Att: 19,760   Gascoigne 4 (1 pen), Lineker

2nd Round (2nd leg)
Oct 9 vs Hartlepool Utd. (a) 2-1 (agg. 7-1)
Att: 9,631   Stewart 2

3rd Round
Oct 30 vs Bradford City (h) 2-1
Att: 25,451   Stewart, Gascoigne

4th Round
Nov 27 vs Sheffield United (a) 2-0
Att: 25,852   Gascoigne, Stewart

5th Round
Jan 16 vs Chelsea (h) 0-0
Att: 34,178

Replay
Jan 23 vs Chelsea (h) 0-3
Att: 33,861

1991/92 SEASON

2nd Round (1st leg)
Sep 25 vs Swansea City (a) 0-1
Att: 11,416

2nd Round (2nd leg)
Oct 9 vs Swansea City (h) 5-1 (agg. 5-2)
Att: 20,198   Stewart, Samways, Lineker, Allen, Brazil (og)

3rd Round
Oct 29 vs Grimsby Town (a) 3-0
Att: 17,017   Howells, Durie, Lineker

4th Round
Dec 4 vs Coventry City (a) 2-1
Att: 20,095   Durie, Allen

5th Round
Jan 8 vs Norwich City (h) 2-1
Att: 29,471   Walsh, Lineker

Semi-Final (1st leg)
Feb 9 vs Nottingham Forest (a) 1-1
Att: 21,402   Lineker (pen)

Semi-Final (2nd leg)
Mar 1 vs Nottingham F. (h) 1-2 (agg. 2-3)
Att: 28,216   Lineker

1992/93 SEASON

2nd Round (1st leg)
Sep 21 vs Brentford (h) 3-1
Att: 19,365   Sheringham, Watson, Durie

2nd Round (2nd leg)
Oct 7 vs Brentford (a) 4-2 (aggregate 7-3)
Att: 11,445   Sheringham 2 (1 pen), Turner, Anderton

3rd Round
Oct 28 vs Manchester City (a) 1-0
Att: 18,399   Samways

4th Round
Dec 2 vs Nottingham Forest (a) 0-2
Att: 22,812

1993/94 SEASON

2nd Round (1st leg)
Sep 22 vs Burnley (a) 0-0
Att: 16,844

2nd Round (2nd leg)
Oct 6 vs Burnley (h) 3-1 (aggregate 3-1)
Att: 20,614   Sheringham 2, Howells

3rd Round
Oct 27 vs Derby County (a) 1-0
Att: 19,855   Barmby

4th Round
Dec 1 vs Blackburn Rovers (h) 1-0
Att: 22,295   Campbell

5th Round
Jan 12 vs Aston Villa (h) 1-2
Att: 31,408   Caskey

1994/95 SEASON

2nd Round (1st leg)
Sep 21 vs Watford (a) 6-3
Att: 13,659   Anderton, Klinsmann 3, Sheringham, Dumitrescu

2nd Round (2nd leg)
Oct 4 vs Watford (h) 2-3 (aggregate 8-6)
Att: 17,798   Barmby, Klinsmann

3rd Round
Oct 26 vs Notts County (a) 0-3
Att: 16,952

1995/96 SEASON

2nd Round (1st leg)
Sep 20 vs Chester City (h) 4-0
Att: 17,645   Armstrong 2, Sheringham, Rosenthal

2nd Round (2nd leg)
Oct 4 vs Chester City (a) 3-1 (agg. 7-1)
Att: 5,372   Sheringham 2, Howells

3rd Round
Oct 25 vs Coventry City (a) 2-3
Att: 18,227   Armstrong, Busst (og)

1996/97 SEASON

2nd Round (1st leg)
Sep 17 vs Preston North End (a) 1-1
Att: 16,258   Anderton

2nd Round (2nd leg)
Sep 25 vs Preston N.E. (h) 3-0 (agg. 4-1)
Att: 20,080   Anderton, Allen 2

3rd Round
Oct 23 vs Sunderland (h) 2-1
Att: 24,867   Armstrong, Campbell

4th Round
Nov 27 vs Bolton Wanderers (a) 1-6
Att: 18,621   Sheringham

1997/98 SEASON

2nd Round (1st leg)
Sep 17 vs Carlisle United (h) 3-2
Att: 19,255   Fenn, Fox, Mahorn

2nd Round (2nd leg)
Sep 30 vs Carlisle United (a) 2-0
Att: 13,571   Ginola (pen), Armstrong

3rd Round
Oct 15 vs Derby County (h) 1-2
Att: 20,390   Ginola

1998/99 SEASON

2nd Round (1st leg)
Sep 15 vs Brentford (a) 3-2
Att: 11,831   Carr, Dominguez, Vega

2nd Round (2nd leg)
Sep 23 vs Brentford (h) 3-2 (aggregate 6-4)
Att: 22,980   Nielsen, Campbell, Armstrong

3rd Round
Oct 27 vs Northampton Town (a) 3-1
Att: 7,422   Armstrong 2, Campbell

4th Round
Nov 10 vs Liverpool (a) 3-1
Att: 20,772   Iversen, Scales, Nielsen

5th Round
Dec 2 vs Manchester United (h) 3-1
Att: 35,702   Armstrong 2, Ginola

Semi-Final (1st leg)
Jan 27 vs Wimbledon (h) 0-0
Att: 35,997

Semi-Final (2nd leg)
Feb 16 vs Wimbledon (a) 1-0 (agg. 1-0)
Att: 25,204   Iversen

FINAL (at Wembley)
Mar 21 vs Leicester City 1-0
Att: 77,892   Nielsen

1999/2000 SEASON

3rd Round
Oct 13 vs Crewe Alexandra (h) 3-1
Att: 25,486   Leonhardsen, Ginola, Sherwood

4th Round
Dec 1 vs Fulham (a) 1-3
Att: 18,134   Iversen

2000/2001 SEASON

2nd Round (1st leg)
Sep 19 vs Brentford (a) 0-0
Att: 8,580

2nd Round (2nd leg)
Sep 26 vs Brentford (h) 2-0 (aggregate 2-0)
Att: 26,909   Leonhardsen, Iversen

3rd Round
Oct 31 vs Birmingham City (h) 1-3
Att: 27,096   Anderton (pen)

2001/2002 SEASON

2nd Round
Sep 13 vs Torquay United (h) 2-0
Att: 20,347   King, Ferdinand

3rd Round
Oct 9 vs Tranmere Rovers (a) 4-0
Att: 12,386   Sheringham (pen), Anderton, Poyet, Rebrov

4th Round
Nov 29 vs Fulham (a) 2-1
Att: 17,006   Rebrov, Davies

5th Round
Dec 11 vs Bolton Wanderers (h) 6-0
Att: 28,430   Davies, Ferdinand 3, Barness (og), Iversen

Semi-Final (1st leg)
Jan 9 vs Chelsea (a) 1-2
Att: 37,264   Ferdinand

Semi-Final (2nd leg)
Jan 23 vs Chelsea (h) 5-1 (aggregate 6-3)
Att: 36,100   Iversen, Sherwood, Sheringham,

Davies, Rebrov
FINAL (at The Millennium Stadium)
Feb 24 vs Blackburn Rovers 1-2
Att: 72,500 Ziege

2002/2003 SEASON
2nd Round
Sep 24 vs Cardiff City (h) 1-0
Att: 23,723 Sheringham

3rd Round
Nov 6 vs Burnley (a) 1-2
Att: 13,512 Poyet

2003/2004 SEASON
2nd Round
Sep 24 vs Coventry City (a) 3-0
Att: 15,474 Kanoute, Keane, Ricketts

3rd Round
Oct 29 vs West Ham United (h) 1-0 (aet)
Att: 36,053 Zamora

4th Round
Dec 3 vs Manchester City (h) 3-1
Att: 31,727 Anderton, Postiga, Kanoute

5th Round
Dec 17 vs Middlesbrough (h) 1-1 (aet)
Att: 25,307 Anderton
Middlesbrough won 5-4 on penalties

UEFA CUP COMPETITION

1983/84 SEASON
1st Round (1st leg)
Sep 14 vs Drogheda (a) 6-0
Att: 7,000 Falco 2, Crooks, Galvin, Mabbutt 2

1st Round (2nd leg)
Sep 28 vs Drogheda (h) 8-0 (agg. 14-0)
Att: 19,891 Falco 2, Roberts 2, Brazil 2, Archibald, Hughton

2nd Round (1st leg)
Oct 19 vs Feyenoord (h) 4-2
Att: 35,404 Archibald 2, Galvin 2

2nd Round (2nd leg)
Nov 2 vs Feyenoord (a) 2-0 (aggregate 6-2)
Att: 45,061 Hughton, Galvin

3rd Round (1st leg)
Nov 23 vs Bayern Munich (a) 0-1
Att: 20,000

3rd Round (2nd leg)
Dec 7 vs Bayern Munich (h) 2-0 (agg. 2-1)
Att: 41,977 Archibald, Falco

Quarter-Final (1st leg)
Mar 7 vs Austria Vienna (h) 2-0
Att: 34,069 Archibald, Brazil

Quarter-Final (2nd leg)
Mar 21 vs Austria Vienna (a) 2-2 (agg. 4-2)
Att: 31,000 Brazil, Ardiles

Semi-Final (1st leg)
Apr 11 vs Hajduk Split (a) 1-2
Att: 40,000 Falco

Semi-Final (2nd leg)
Apr 25 vs Hajduk Split (h) 1-0 (agg. 2-2)
Att: 43,969 Hazard
Tottenham won on the away goals rule

FINAL (1st leg)
May 9 vs Anderlecht (a) 1-1
Att: 40,000 Miller

FINAL (2nd leg)
May 23 vs Anderlecht (h) 1-1 (aet) (agg. 2-2)
Att: 46,205 Roberts
Tottenham won 4-3 on penalties

1984/85 SEASON
1st Round (1st leg)
Sep 19 vs Sporting Braga (a) 3-0
Att: 26,000 Falco 2, Galvin

1st Round (2nd leg)
Oct 3 vs Sporting Braga (h) 6-0 (agg. 9-0)
Att: 22,478 Stevens, Hughton, Crooks 3, Falco

2nd Round (1st leg)
Oct 24 vs FC Brugge (a) 1-2
Att: 27,000 Allen

2nd Round (2nd leg)
Nov 7 vs FC Brugge (h) 3-0 (agg. 4-2)
Att: 34,356 Hazard, Allen, Roberts

3rd Round (1st leg)
Nov 28 vs Bohemians Prague (h) 2-0
Att: 27,951 Ondra (og), Stevens

3rd Round (2nd leg)
Dec 12 vs Bohem. Prague (a) 1-1 (agg. 3-1)
Att: 17,500 Falco

Quarter-Final (1st leg)
Mar 6 vs Real Madrid (h) 0-1
Att: 39,914

Quarter-Final (2nd leg)
Mar 20 vs Real Madrid (a) 0-0 (agg. 0-1)
Att: 95,000

1999/2000 SEASON
1st Round (1st leg)
Sep 16 vs Zimbru Chisinau (h) 3-0
Att: 32,660 Leonhardsen, Perry, Sherwood

1st Round (2nd leg)
Sep 30 vs Zimbru Chisinau (a) 0-0 (agg 3-0)
Att: 7,000

2nd Round (1st leg)
Oct 28 vs Kaiserslautern (h) 1-0
Att: 35,177 Iversen (pen)

2nd Round (2nd leg)
Nov 4 vs Kaiserslautern (a) 0-2 (agg. 1-2)
Att: 29,044

CUP-WINNERS' CUP

1981/82 SEASON
1st Round (1st leg)
Sep 16 vs Ajax (a) 3-1
Att: 27,500 Falco 2, Villa

1st Round (2nd leg)
Sep 29 vs Ajax (h) 3-0 (aggregate 6-1)
Att: 34,606 Galvin, Falco, Ardiles

2nd Round (1st leg)
Oct 21 vs Dundalk (a) 1-1
Att: 17,000 Crooks

2nd Round (2nd leg)
Nov 4 vs Dundalk (h) 1-0 (aggregate 2-1)
Att: 33,455 Crooks

Quarter-Final (1st leg)
Mar 3 vs Eintracht Frankfurt (h) 2-0
Att: 38,172 Miller, Hazard

Quarter-Final (2nd leg)
Mar 17 vs Eint. Frankfurt (a) 1-2 (agg. 3-2)
Att: 41,000 Hoddle

Semi-Final (1st leg)
Apr 7 vs Barcelona (h) 1-1
Att: 41,555 Roberts

Semi-Final (2nd leg)
Apr 21 vs Barcelona (a) 0-1 (aggregate 1-2)
Att: 80,000

1982/83 SEASON
1st Round (1st leg)
Sep 15 vs Coleraine (a) 3-0
Att: 12,000 Archibald, Crooks 2

1st Round (2nd leg)
Sep 28 vs Coleraine (h) 4-0 (aggregate 7-0)
Att: 20,925 Crooks, Mabbutt, Brooke, Gibson

2nd Round (1st leg)
Oct 20 vs Bayern Munich (h) 1-1
Att: 36,488 Archibald

2nd Round (2nd leg)
Nov 3 vs Bayern Munich (a) 1-4 (agg. 2-5)
Att: 50,000 Hughton

1991/92 SEASON
Preliminary Round (1st leg)
Aug 21 vs Sparkasse Stockerau (a) 1-0
Att: 15,500 Durie

Preliminary Round (2nd leg)
Sep 4 vs Spark. Stockerau (h) 1-0 (agg. 2-0)
Att: 28,072 Mabbutt

1st Round (1st leg)
Sep 17 vs Hajduk Split (a) 0-1
Att: 7,000

1st Round (2nd leg)
Oct 2 vs Hajduk Split (h) 2-0 (agg. 2-1)
Att: 24,297 Tuttle, Durie

2nd Round (1st leg)
Oct 23 vs FC Porto (h) 3-1
Att: 23,621 Lineker 2, Durie

2nd Round (2nd leg)
Nov 7 vs FC Porto (a) 0-0 (aggregate 3-1)
Att: 55,000

Quarter-Final (1st leg)
Mar 4 vs Feyenoord (a) 0-1
Att: 48,000

Quarter-Final (2nd leg)
Mar 18 vs Feyenoord (h) 0-0 (agg. 0-1)
Att: 29,834

Season 1974/75

DIVISION ONE

Derby County	42	21	11	10	67	49	53
Liverpool	42	20	11	11	60	39	51
Ipswich Town	42	23	5	14	66	44	51
Everton	42	16	18	8	56	42	50
Stoke City	42	17	15	10	64	48	49
Sheffield United	42	18	13	11	58	51	49
Middlesbrough	42	18	12	12	54	40	48
Manchester City	42	18	10	14	54	54	46
Leeds United	42	16	13	13	57	49	45
Burnley	42	17	11	14	68	67	45
Queen's Park Rangers	42	16	10	16	54	54	42
Wolverhampton Wanderers	42	14	11	17	57	54	39
West Ham United	42	13	13	16	58	59	39
Coventry City	42	12	15	15	51	62	39
Newcastle United	42	15	9	18	59	72	39
Arsenal	42	13	11	18	47	49	37
Birmingham City	42	14	9	19	53	61	37
Leicester City	42	12	12	18	46	60	36
Tottenham Hotspur	**42**	**13**	**8**	**21**	**52**	**63**	**34**
Luton Town	42	11	11	20	47	65	33
Chelsea	42	9	15	18	42	72	33
Carlisle United	42	12	5	25	43	59	29

Season 1975/76

DIVISION ONE

Liverpool	42	23	14	5	66	31	60
Queen's Park Rangers	42	24	11	7	67	33	59
Manchester United	42	23	10	9	68	42	56
Derby County	42	21	11	10	75	58	53
Leeds United	42	21	9	12	65	46	51
Ipswich Town	42	16	14	12	54	48	46
Leicester City	42	13	19	10	48	51	45
Manchester City	42	16	11	15	64	46	43
Tottenham Hotspur	**42**	**14**	**15**	**13**	**63**	**63**	**43**
Norwich City	42	16	10	16	58	58	42
Everton	42	15	12	15	60	66	42
Stoke City	42	15	11	16	48	50	41
Middlesbrough	42	15	10	17	46	45	40
Coventry City	42	13	14	15	47	57	40
Newcastle United	42	15	9	18	71	62	39
Aston Villa	42	11	17	14	51	59	39
Arsenal	42	13	10	19	47	53	36
West Ham United	42	13	10	19	48	71	36
Birmingham City	42	13	7	22	57	75	33
Wolverhampton Wanderers	42	10	10	22	51	68	30
Burnley	42	9	10	23	43	66	28
Sheffield United	42	6	10	26	33	82	22

Season 1976/77

DIVISION ONE

Liverpool	42	23	11	8	62	33	57
Manchester City	42	21	14	7	60	34	56
Ipswich Town	42	22	8	12	66	39	52
Aston Villa	42	22	7	13	76	50	51
Newcastle United	42	18	13	11	64	49	49
Manchester United	42	18	11	13	71	62	47
West Bromwich Albion	42	16	13	13	62	56	45
Arsenal	42	16	11	15	64	59	43
Everton	42	14	14	14	62	64	42
Leeds United	42	15	12	15	48	51	42
Leicester City	42	12	18	12	47	60	42
Middlesbrough	42	14	13	15	40	45	41
Birmingham City	42	13	12	17	63	61	38
Queen's Park Rangers	42	13	12	17	47	52	38
Derby County	42	9	19	14	50	55	37
Norwich City	42	14	9	19	47	64	37
West Ham United	42	11	14	17	46	65	36
Bristol City	42	11	13	18	38	48	35
Coventry City	42	10	15	17	48	59	35
Sunderland	42	11	12	19	46	54	34
Stoke City	42	10	14	18	28	51	34
Tottenham Hotspur	**42**	**12**	**9**	**21**	**48**	**72**	**33**

Season 1977/78

DIVISION TWO

Bolton Wanderers	42	24	10	8	63	33	58
Southampton	42	22	13	7	70	39	57
Tottenham Hotspur	**42**	**20**	**16**	**6**	**83**	**49**	**56**
Brighton & Hove Albion	42	22	12	8	63	38	56
Blackburn Rovers	42	16	13	13	56	60	45
Sunderland	42	14	16	12	67	59	44
Stoke City	42	16	10	16	53	49	42
Oldham Athletic	42	13	16	13	54	58	42
Crystal Palace	42	13	15	14	50	47	41
Fulham	42	14	13	15	49	49	41
Burnley	42	15	10	17	56	64	40
Sheffield United	42	16	8	18	62	73	40
Luton Town	42	14	10	18	54	52	38
Orient	42	10	18	14	43	49	38
Notts County	42	11	16	15	54	62	38
Millwall	42	12	14	16	49	57	38
Charlton Athletic	42	13	12	17	55	68	38
Bristol Rovers	42	13	12	17	61	77	38
Cardiff City	42	13	12	17	51	71	38
Blackpool	42	12	13	17	59	60	37
Mansfield Town	42	10	11	21	49	69	31
Hull City	42	8	12	22	34	52	28

Season 1978/79

DIVISION ONE

Liverpool	42	30	8	4	85	16	68
Nottingham Forest	42	21	18	3	61	26	60
West Bromwich Albion	42	24	11	7	72	35	59
Everton	42	17	17	8	52	40	51
Leeds United	42	18	14	10	70	52	50
Ipswich Town	42	20	9	13	63	49	49
Arsenal	42	17	14	11	61	48	48
Aston Villa	42	15	16	11	59	49	46
Manchester United	42	15	15	12	60	63	45
Coventry City	42	14	16	12	58	68	44
Tottenham Hotspur	**42**	**13**	**15**	**14**	**48**	**61**	**41**
Middlesbrough	42	15	10	17	57	50	40
Bristol City	42	15	10	17	47	51	40
Southampton	42	12	16	14	47	53	40
Manchester City	42	13	13	16	58	56	39
Norwich City	42	7	23	12	51	57	37
Bolton Wanderers	42	12	11	19	54	75	35
Wolverhampton Wands.	42	13	8	21	44	68	34
Derby County	42	10	11	21	44	71	31
Queen's Park Rangers	42	6	13	23	45	73	25
Birmingham City	42	6	10	26	37	64	22
Chelsea	42	5	10	27	44	92	20

Season 1979/80

DIVISION ONE

Liverpool	42	25	10	7	81	30	60
Manchester United	42	24	10	8	65	35	58
Ispwich	42	22	9	11	68	39	53
Arsenal	42	18	16	8	52	36	52
Nottingham Forest	42	20	8	14	63	43	48
Wolverhampton Wands.	42	19	9	14	58	47	47
Aston Villa	42	16	14	12	51	50	46
Southampton	42	18	9	15	65	53	45
Middlesbrough	42	16	12	14	50	44	44
West Bromwich Albion	42	11	19	12	54	50	41
Leeds United	42	13	14	15	46	50	40
Norwich City	42	13	14	15	58	66	40
Crystal Palace	42	12	16	14	41	50	40
Tottenham Hotspur	**42**	**15**	**10**	**17**	**52**	**62**	**40**
Coventry City	42	16	7	19	56	66	39
Brighton & Hove Albion	42	11	15	16	47	57	37
Manchester City	42	12	13	17	43	66	37
Stoke City	42	13	10	19	44	58	36
Everton	42	9	17	16	43	51	35
Bristol City	42	9	13	20	37	66	31
Derby County	42	11	8	23	47	67	30
Bolton Wanderers	42	5	15	22	38	73	25

91

Season 1980/81

DIVISION ONE

Aston Villa	42	26	8	8	72	40	60
Ipswich Town	42	23	10	9	77	43	56
Arsenal	42	19	15	8	61	45	53
West Bromwich Albion	42	20	12	10	60	42	52
Liverpool	42	17	17	8	62	42	51
Southampton	42	20	10	12	76	56	50
Nottingham Forest	42	19	12	11	62	44	50
Manchester United	42	15	18	9	51	36	48
Leeds United	42	17	10	15	39	47	44
Tottenham Hotspur	**42**	**14**	**15**	**13**	**70**	**68**	**43**
Stoke City	42	12	18	12	51	60	42
Manchester City	42	14	11	17	56	59	39
Birmingham City	42	13	12	17	50	61	38
Middlesbrough	42	16	5	21	53	61	37
Everton	42	13	10	19	55	58	36
Coventry City	42	13	10	19	48	68	36
Sunderland	42	14	7	21	52	53	35
Wolverhampton Wands.	42	13	9	20	43	55	35
Brighton & Hove Albion	42	14	7	21	54	67	35
Norwich City	42	13	7	22	49	73	33
Leicester City	42	13	6	23	40	67	32
Crystal Palace	42	6	7	29	47	83	19

Season 1981/82

DIVISION ONE

Liverpool	42	26	9	7	80	32	87
Ipswich Town	42	26	5	11	75	53	83
Manchester United	42	22	12	8	59	29	78
Tottenham Hotspur	**42**	**20**	**11**	**11**	**67**	**48**	**71**
Arsenal	42	20	11	11	48	37	71
Swansea City	42	21	6	15	58	51	69
Southampton	42	19	9	14	72	67	66
Everton	42	17	13	12	56	50	64
West Ham United	42	14	16	12	66	57	58
Manchester City	42	15	13	14	49	50	58
Aston Villa	42	15	12	15	55	53	57
Nottingham Forest	42	15	12	15	42	48	57
Brighton & Hove Albion	42	13	13	16	43	52	52
Coventry City	42	13	11	18	56	62	50
Notts County	42	13	8	21	61	69	47
Birmingham City	42	10	14	18	53	61	44
West Bromwich Albion	42	11	11	20	46	57	44
Stoke City	42	12	8	22	44	63	44
Sunderland	42	11	11	20	38	58	44
Leeds United	42	10	12	20	39	61	42
Wolverhampton Wands.	42	10	10	22	32	63	40
Middlesbrough	42	8	15	19	34	52	39

Season 1982/83

DIVISION ONE

Liverpool	42	24	10	8	87	37	82
Watford	42	22	5	15	74	57	71
Manchester United	42	19	13	10	56	38	70
Tottenham Hotspur	**42**	**20**	**9**	**13**	**65**	**50**	**69**
Nottingham Forest	42	20	9	13	62	50	69
Aston Villa	42	21	5	16	62	50	68
Everton	42	18	10	14	66	48	64
West Ham United	42	20	4	18	68	62	64
Ipswich Town	42	15	13	14	64	50	58
Arsenal	42	16	10	16	58	56	58
West Bromwich Albion	42	15	12	15	51	49	57
Southampton	42	15	12	15	54	58	57
Stoke City	42	16	9	17	53	64	57
Norwich City	42	14	12	16	52	58	54
Notts County	42	15	7	20	55	71	52
Sunderland	42	12	14	16	48	61	50
Birmingham City	42	12	14	16	40	55	50
Luton Town	42	12	13	17	65	84	49
Coventry City	42	13	9	20	48	59	48
Manchester City	42	13	8	21	47	70	47
Swansea City	42	10	11	21	51	69	41
Brighton & Hove Albion	42	9	13	20	38	68	40

Season 1983/84

DIVISION ONE

Liverpool	42	22	14	6	73	32	80
Southampton	42	22	11	9	66	38	77
Nottingham Forest	42	22	8	12	76	45	74
Manchester United	42	20	14	8	71	41	74
Queen's Park Rangers	42	22	7	13	67	37	73
Arsenal	42	18	9	15	74	60	63
Everton	42	16	14	12	44	42	62
Tottenham Hotspur	**42**	**17**	**10**	**15**	**64**	**65**	**61**
West Ham United	42	17	9	16	60	55	60
Aston Villa	42	17	9	16	59	61	60
Watford	42	16	9	17	68	77	57
Ipswich Town	42	15	8	19	55	57	53
Sunderland	42	13	13	16	42	53	52
Norwich City	42	12	15	15	48	49	51
Leicester City	42	13	12	17	65	68	51
Luton Town	42	14	9	19	53	66	51
West Bromwich Albion	42	14	9	19	48	62	51
Stoke City	42	13	11	18	44	63	50
Coventry City	42	13	11	18	57	77	50
Birmingham City	42	12	12	18	39	50	48
Notts County	42	10	11	21	50	72	41
Wolverhampton Wands.	42	6	11	25	27	80	29

Season 1984/85

DIVISION ONE

Everton	42	28	6	8	88	43	90
Liverpool	42	22	11	9	68	35	77
Tottenham Hotspur	**42**	**23**	**8**	**11**	**78**	**51**	**77**
Manchester United	42	22	10	10	77	47	76
Southampton	42	19	11	12	56	47	68
Chelsea	42	18	12	12	63	48	66
Arsenal	42	19	9	14	61	49	66
Sheffield Wednesday	42	17	14	11	58	45	65
Nottingham Forest	42	19	7	16	56	48	64
Aston Villa	42	15	11	16	60	60	56
Watford	42	14	13	15	81	71	55
West Bromwich Albion	42	16	7	19	58	62	55
Luton Town	42	15	9	18	57	61	54
Newcastle United	42	13	13	16	55	70	52
Leicester City	42	15	6	21	65	73	51
West Ham United	42	13	12	17	51	68	51
Ipswich Town	42	13	11	18	46	57	50
Coventry City	42	15	5	22	47	64	50
Queen's Park Rangers	42	13	11	18	53	72	50
Norwich City	42	13	10	19	46	64	49
Sunderland	42	10	10	22	40	62	40
Stoke City	42	3	8	31	24	91	17

Season 1985/86

DIVISION ONE

Liverpool	42	26	10	6	89	37	88
Everton	42	26	8	8	87	41	86
West Ham United	42	26	6	10	74	40	84
Manchester United	42	22	10	10	70	36	76
Sheffield Wednesday	42	21	10	11	63	54	73
Chelsea	42	20	11	11	57	56	71
Arsenal	42	20	9	13	49	47	69
Nottingham Forest	42	19	11	12	69	53	68
Luton Town	42	18	12	12	61	44	66
Tottenham Hotspur	**42**	**19**	**8**	**15**	**74**	**52**	**65**
Newcastle United	42	17	12	13	67	72	63
Watford	42	16	11	15	69	62	59
Queen's Park Rangers	42	15	7	20	53	64	52
Southampton	42	12	10	20	51	62	46
Manchester City	42	11	12	19	43	57	45
Aston Villa	42	10	14	18	51	67	44
Coventry City	42	11	10	21	48	71	43
Oxford United	42	10	12	20	62	80	42
Leicester City	42	10	12	20	54	76	42
Ipswich Town	42	11	8	23	32	55	41
Birmingham City	42	8	5	29	30	73	29
West Bromwich Albion	42	4	12	26	35	89	24

Season 1986/87

DIVISION ONE

	P	W	D	L	F	A	Pts
Everton	42	26	8	8	76	31	86
Liverpool	42	23	8	11	72	42	77
Tottenham Hotspur	42	21	8	13	68	43	71
Arsenal	42	20	10	12	58	35	70
Norwich City	42	17	17	8	53	51	68
Wimbledon	42	19	9	14	57	50	66
Luton Town	42	18	12	12	47	45	66
Nottingham Forest	42	18	11	13	64	51	65
Watford	42	18	9	15	67	54	63
Coventry City	42	17	12	13	50	45	63
Manchester United	42	14	14	14	52	45	56
Southampton	42	14	10	18	69	68	52
Sheffield Wednesday	42	13	13	16	58	59	52
Chelsea	42	13	13	16	53	64	52
West Ham United	42	14	10	18	52	67	52
Queen's Park Rangers	42	13	11	18	48	64	50
Newcastle United	42	12	11	19	47	65	47
Oxford United	42	11	13	18	44	69	46
Charlton Athletic	42	11	11	20	45	55	44
Leicester City	42	11	9	22	54	76	42
Manchester City	42	8	15	19	36	57	39
Aston Villa	42	8	12	22	45	79	36

Season 1987/88

DIVISION ONE

	P	W	D	L	F	A	Pts
Liverpool	40	26	12	2	87	24	90
Manchester United	40	23	12	5	71	38	81
Nottingham Forest	40	20	13	7	67	39	73
Everton	40	19	13	8	53	27	70
Queen's Park Rangers	40	19	10	11	48	38	67
Arsenal	40	18	12	10	58	39	66
Wimbledon	40	14	15	11	58	47	57
Newcastle United	40	14	14	12	55	53	56
Luton Town	40	14	11	15	57	58	53
Coventry City	40	13	14	13	46	53	53
Sheffield Wednesday	40	15	8	17	52	66	53
Southampton	40	12	14	14	49	53	50
Tottenham Hotspur	40	12	11	17	38	48	47
Norwich City	40	12	9	19	40	52	45
Derby County	40	10	13	17	35	45	43
West Ham United	40	9	15	16	40	52	42
Charlton Athletic	40	9	15	16	38	52	42
Chelsea	40	9	15	16	50	68	42
Portsmouth	40	7	14	19	36	66	35
Watford	40	7	11	22	27	51	32
Oxford United	40	6	13	21	44	80	31

Season 1988/89

DIVISION ONE

	P	W	D	L	F	A	Pts
Arsenal	38	22	10	6	73	36	76
Liverpool	38	22	10	6	65	28	76
Nottingham Forest	38	17	13	8	64	43	64
Norwich City	38	17	11	10	48	45	62
Derby County	38	17	7	14	40	38	58
Tottenham Hotspur	38	15	12	11	60	46	57
Coventry City	38	14	13	11	47	42	55
Everton	38	14	12	12	50	45	54
Queen's Park Rangers	38	14	11	13	43	37	53
Millwall	38	14	11	13	47	52	53
Manchester United	38	13	12	13	45	35	51
Wimbledon	38	14	9	15	50	46	51
Southampton	38	10	15	13	52	66	45
Charlton Athletic	38	10	12	16	44	58	42
Sheffield Wednesday	38	10	12	16	34	51	42
Luton Town	38	10	11	17	42	52	41
Aston Villa	38	9	13	16	45	56	40
Middlesbrough	38	9	12	17	44	61	39
West Ham United	38	10	8	20	37	62	38
Newcastle United	38	7	10	21	32	63	31

Season 1989/90

DIVISION ONE

	P	W	D	L	F	A	Pts
Liverpool	38	23	10	5	78	37	79
Aston Villa	38	21	7	10	57	38	70
Tottenham Hotspur	38	19	6	13	59	47	63
Arsenal	38	18	8	12	54	38	62
Chelsea	38	16	12	10	58	50	60
Everton	38	17	8	13	57	46	59
Southampton	38	15	10	13	71	63	55
Wimbledon	38	13	16	9	47	40	55
Nottingham Forest	38	15	9	14	55	47	54
Norwich City	38	13	14	11	44	42	53
Queen's Park Rangers	38	13	11	14	45	44	50
Coventry City	38	14	7	17	39	59	49
Manchester United	38	13	9	16	46	47	48
Manchester City	38	12	12	14	43	52	48
Crystal Palace	38	13	9	16	42	66	48
Derby County	38	13	7	18	43	40	46
Luton Town	38	10	13	15	43	57	43
Sheffield Wednesday	38	11	10	17	35	51	43
Charlton Athletic	38	7	9	22	31	57	30
Millwall	38	5	11	22	39	65	26

Season 1990/91

DIVISION ONE

	P	W	D	L	F	A	Pts
Arsenal	38	24	13	1	74	18	83
Liverpool	38	23	7	8	77	40	76
Crystal Palace	38	20	9	9	50	41	69
Leeds United	38	19	7	12	65	47	64
Manchester City	38	17	11	10	64	53	62
Manchester United	38	16	12	10	58	45	60
Wimbledon	38	14	14	10	53	46	56
Nottingham Forest	38	14	12	12	65	50	54
Everton	38	13	12	13	50	46	51
Tottenham Hotspur	38	11	16	11	51	50	49
Chelsea	38	13	10	15	58	69	49
Queen's Park Rangers	38	12	10	16	44	53	46
Sheffield United	38	13	7	18	36	55	46
Southampton	38	12	9	17	58	69	45
Norwich City	38	13	6	19	41	64	45
Coventry City	38	11	11	16	42	49	44
Aston Villa	38	9	14	15	46	58	41
Luton Town	38	10	7	21	42	61	37
Sunderland	38	8	10	20	38	60	34
Derby County	38	5	9	24	37	75	24

Arsenal had 2 points deducted
Manchester United had 1 point deducted

Season 1991/92

DIVISION ONE

	P	W	D	L	F	A	Pts
Leeds United	42	22	16	4	74	37	82
Manchester United	42	21	15	6	63	33	78
Sheffield Wednesday	42	21	12	9	62	49	75
Arsenal	42	19	15	8	81	46	72
Manchester City	42	20	10	12	61	48	70
Liverpool	42	16	16	10	47	40	64
Aston Villa	42	17	9	16	48	44	60
Nottingham Forest	42	16	11	15	60	58	59
Sheffield United	42	16	9	17	65	63	57
Crystal Palace	42	14	15	13	53	61	57
Queen's Park Rangers	42	12	18	12	48	47	54
Everton	42	13	14	15	52	51	53
Wimbledon	42	13	14	15	53	53	53
Chelsea	42	13	14	15	50	60	53
Tottenham Hotspur	42	15	7	20	58	63	52
Southampton	42	14	10	18	39	55	52
Oldham Athletic	42	14	9	19	63	67	51
Norwich City	42	11	12	19	47	63	45
Coventry City	42	11	11	20	35	44	44
Luton Town	42	10	12	20	38	71	42
Notts County	42	10	10	22	40	62	40
West Ham United	42	9	11	22	37	59	38

Season 1992/93
F.A. PREMIER LEAGUE

Manchester United	42	24	12	6	67	31	84
Aston Villa	42	21	11	10	57	40	74
Norwich City	42	21	9	12	61	65	72
Blackburn Rovers	42	20	11	11	68	46	71
Queen's Park Rangers	42	17	12	13	63	55	63
Liverpool	42	16	11	15	62	55	59
Sheffield Wednesday	42	15	14	13	55	51	59
Tottenham Hotspur	**42**	**16**	**11**	**15**	**60**	**66**	**59**
Manchester City	42	15	12	15	56	51	57
Arsenal	42	15	11	16	40	38	56
Chelsea	42	14	14	14	51	54	56
Wimbledon	42	14	12	16	56	55	54
Everton	42	15	8	19	53	55	53
Sheffield United	42	14	10	18	54	53	52
Coventry City	42	13	13	16	52	57	52
Ipswich Town	42	12	16	14	50	55	52
Leeds United	42	12	15	15	57	62	51
Southampton	42	13	11	18	54	61	50
Oldham Athletic	42	13	10	19	63	74	49
Crystal Palace	42	11	16	15	48	61	49
Middlesbrough	42	11	11	20	54	75	44
Nottingham Forest	42	10	10	22	41	62	40

Season 1993/94
F.A.PREMIERSHIP

Manchester United	42	27	11	4	80	38	92
Blackburn Rovers	42	25	9	8	63	36	84
Newcastle United	42	23	8	11	82	41	77
Arsenal	42	18	17	7	53	28	71
Leeds United	42	18	16	8	65	39	70
Wimbledon	42	18	11	13	56	53	65
Sheffield Wednesday	42	16	16	10	76	54	64
Liverpool	42	17	9	16	59	55	60
Queen's Park Rangers	42	16	12	14	62	61	60
Aston Villa	42	15	12	15	46	50	57
Coventry City	42	14	14	14	43	45	56
Norwich City	42	12	17	13	65	61	53
West Ham United	42	13	13	16	47	58	52
Chelsea	42	13	12	17	49	53	51
Tottenham Hotspur	**42**	**11**	**12**	**19**	**54**	**59**	**45**
Manchester City	42	9	18	15	38	49	45
Everton	42	12	8	22	42	63	44
Southampton	42	12	7	23	49	66	43
Ipswich Town	42	9	16	17	35	58	43
Sheffield United	42	8	18	16	42	60	42
Oldham Athletic	42	9	13	20	42	68	40
Swindon Town	42	5	15	22	47	100	30

Season 1994/95
F.A. PREMIERSHIP

Blackburn Rovers	42	27	8	7	80	39	89
Manchester United	42	26	10	6	77	28	88
Nottingham Forest	42	22	11	9	72	43	77
Liverpool	42	21	11	10	65	37	74
Leeds United	42	20	13	9	59	38	73
Newcastle United	42	20	12	10	67	47	72
Tottenham Hotspur	**42**	**16**	**14**	**12**	**66**	**58**	**62**
Queen's Park Rangers	42	17	9	16	61	59	60
Wimbledon	42	15	11	16	48	65	56
Southampton	42	12	18	12	61	63	54
Chelsea	42	13	15	14	50	55	54
Arsenal	42	13	12	17	52	49	51
Sheffield Wednesday	42	13	12	17	49	57	51
West Ham United	42	13	11	18	44	48	50
Everton	42	11	17	14	44	51	50
Coventry City	42	12	14	16	44	62	50
Manchester City	42	12	13	17	53	64	49
Aston Villa	42	11	15	16	51	56	48
Crystal Palace	42	11	12	19	34	49	45
Norwich City	42	10	13	19	37	54	43
Leicester City	42	6	11	25	45	80	29
Ipswich Town	42	7	6	29	36	93	27

Season 1995/96
F.A. PREMIERSHIP

Manchester United	38	25	7	6	73	35	82
Newcastle United	38	24	6	8	66	37	78
Liverpool	38	20	11	7	70	34	71
Aston Villa	38	18	9	11	52	35	63
Arsenal	38	17	12	9	49	32	63
Everton	38	17	10	11	64	44	61
Blackburn Rovers	38	18	7	13	61	47	61
Tottenham Hotspur	**38**	**16**	**13**	**9**	**50**	**38**	**61**
Nottingham Forest	38	15	13	10	50	54	58
West Ham United	38	14	9	15	43	52	51
Chelsea	38	12	14	12	46	44	50
Middlesbrough	38	11	10	17	35	50	43
Leeds United	38	12	7	19	40	57	43
Wimbledon	38	10	11	17	55	70	41
Sheffield Wednesday	38	10	10	18	48	61	40
Coventry City	38	8	14	16	42	60	38
Southampton	38	9	11	18	34	52	38
Manchester City	38	9	11	18	33	58	38
Queen's Park Rangers	38	9	6	23	38	57	33
Bolton Wanderers	38	8	5	25	39	71	29

Season 1996/97
F.A. PREMIERSHIP

Manchester United	38	21	12	5	76	44	75
Newcastle United	38	19	11	8	73	40	68
Arsenal	38	19	11	8	62	32	68
Liverpool	38	19	11	8	62	37	68
Aston Villa	38	17	10	11	47	34	61
Chelsea	38	16	11	11	58	55	59
Sheffield Wednesday	38	14	15	9	50	51	57
Wimbledon	38	15	11	12	49	46	56
Leicester City	38	12	11	15	46	54	47
Tottenham Hotspur	**38**	**13**	**7**	**18**	**44**	**51**	**46**
Leeds United	38	11	13	14	28	38	46
Derby County	38	11	13	14	45	58	46
Blackburn Rovers	38	9	15	14	42	43	42
West Ham United	38	10	12	16	39	48	42
Everton	38	10	12	16	44	57	42
Southampton	38	10	11	17	50	56	41
Coventry City	38	9	14	15	38	54	41
Sunderland	38	10	10	18	35	53	40
Middlesbrough	38	10	12	16	51	60	39
Nottingham Forest	38	6	16	16	31	59	34

Middlesbrough had 3 points deducted

Season 1997/98
F.A. PREMIERSHIP

Arsenal	38	23	9	6	68	33	78
Manchester United	38	23	8	7	73	26	77
Liverpool	38	18	11	9	68	42	65
Chelsea	38	20	3	15	71	43	63
Leeds United	38	17	8	13	57	46	59
Blackburn Rovers	38	16	10	12	57	52	58
Aston Villa	38	17	6	15	49	48	57
West Ham United	38	16	8	14	56	57	56
Derby County	38	16	7	15	52	49	55
Leicester City	38	13	14	11	51	41	53
Coventry City	38	12	16	10	46	44	52
Southampton	38	14	6	18	50	55	48
Newcastle United	38	11	11	16	35	44	44
Tottenham Hotspur	**38**	**11**	**11**	**16**	**44**	**56**	**44**
Wimbledon	38	10	14	14	34	46	44
Sheffield Wednesday	38	12	8	18	52	67	44
Everton	38	9	13	16	41	56	40
Bolton Wanderers	38	9	13	16	41	61	40
Barnsley	38	10	5	23	37	82	35
Crystal Palace	38	8	9	21	37	71	33

Season 1998/99

F.A. PREMIERSHIP

Manchester United	38	22	13	3	80	37	79
Arsenal	38	22	12	4	59	17	78
Chelsea	38	20	15	3	57	30	75
Leeds United	38	18	13	7	62	34	67
West Ham United	38	16	9	13	46	53	57
Aston Villa	38	15	10	13	51	46	55
Liverpool	38	15	9	14	68	49	54
Derby County	38	13	13	12	40	45	52
Middlesbrough	38	12	15	11	48	54	51
Leicester City	38	12	13	13	40	46	49
Tottenham Hotspur	**38**	**11**	**14**	**13**	**47**	**50**	**47**
Sheffield Wednesday	38	13	7	18	41	42	46
Newcastle United	38	11	13	14	48	54	46
Everton	38	11	10	17	42	47	43
Coventry City	38	11	9	18	39	51	42
Wimbledon	38	10	12	16	40	63	42
Southampton	38	11	8	19	37	64	41
Charlton Athletic	38	8	12	18	41	56	36
Blackburn Rovers	38	7	14	17	38	52	35
Nottingham Forest	38	7	9	22	35	69	30

Season 1999/2000

F.A. PREMIERSHIP

Manchester United	38	28	7	3	97	45	91
Arsenal	38	22	7	9	73	43	73
Leeds United	38	21	6	11	58	43	69
Liverpool	38	19	10	9	51	30	67
Chelsea	38	18	11	9	53	34	65
Aston Villa	38	15	13	10	46	35	58
Sunderland	38	16	10	12	57	56	58
Leicester City	38	16	7	15	55	55	55
West Ham United	38	15	10	13	52	53	55
Tottenham Hotspur	**38**	**15**	**8**	**15**	**57**	**49**	**53**
Newcastle United	38	14	10	14	63	54	52
Middlesbrough	38	14	10	14	46	52	52
Everton	38	12	14	12	59	49	50
Coventry City	38	12	8	18	47	54	44
Southampton	38	12	8	18	45	62	44
Derby County	38	9	11	18	44	57	38
Bradford City	38	9	9	20	38	68	36
Wimbledon	38	7	12	19	46	74	33
Sheffield Wednesday	38	8	7	23	38	70	31
Watford	38	6	6	26	35	77	24

Season 2000/2001

F.A. PREMIERSHIP

Manchester United	38	24	8	6	79	31	80
Arsenal	38	20	10	8	63	38	70
Liverpool	38	20	9	9	71	39	69
Leeds United	38	20	8	10	64	43	68
Ipswich Town	38	20	6	12	57	42	66
Chelsea	38	17	10	11	68	45	61
Sunderland	38	15	12	11	46	41	57
Aston Villa	38	13	15	10	46	43	54
Charlton Athletic	38	14	10	14	50	57	52
Southampton	38	14	10	14	40	48	52
Newcastle United	38	14	9	15	44	50	51
Tottenham Hotspur	**38**	**13**	**10**	**15**	**47**	**54**	**49**
Leicester City	38	14	6	18	39	51	48
Middlesbrough	38	9	15	14	44	44	42
West Ham United	38	10	12	16	45	50	42
Everton	38	11	9	18	45	59	42
Derby County	38	10	12	16	37	59	42
Manchester City	38	8	10	20	41	65	34
Coventry City	38	8	10	20	36	63	34
Bradford City	38	5	11	22	30	70	26

Season 2001/2002

F.A. PREMIERSHIP

Arsenal	38	26	9	3	79	36	87
Liverpool	38	24	8	6	67	30	80
Manchester United	38	24	5	9	87	45	77
Newcastle United	38	21	8	9	74	52	71
Leeds United	38	18	12	8	53	37	66
Chelsea	38	17	13	8	66	38	64
West Ham United	38	15	8	15	48	57	53
Aston Villa	38	12	14	12	46	47	50
Tottenham Hotspur	**38**	**14**	**8**	**16**	**49**	**53**	**50**
Blackburn Rovers	38	12	10	16	55	51	46
Southampton	38	12	9	17	46	54	45
Middlesbrough	38	12	9	17	35	47	45
Fulham	38	10	14	14	36	44	44
Charlton Athletic	38	10	14	14	38	49	44
Everton	38	11	10	17	45	57	43
Bolton Wanderers	38	9	13	16	44	62	40
Sunderland	38	10	10	18	29	51	40
Ipswich Town	38	9	9	20	41	64	36
Derby County	38	8	6	24	33	63	30
Leicester City	38	5	13	20	30	64	28

Season 2002/2003

F.A. PREMIERSHIP

Manchester United	38	25	8	5	74	34	83
Arsenal	38	23	9	6	85	42	78
Newcastle United	38	21	6	11	63	48	69
Chelsea	38	19	10	9	68	38	67
Liverpool	38	18	10	10	61	41	64
Blackburn Rovers	38	16	12	10	52	43	60
Everton	38	17	8	13	48	49	59
Southampton	38	13	13	12	43	46	52
Manchester City	38	15	6	17	47	54	51
Tottenham Hotspur	**38**	**14**	**8**	**16**	**51**	**62**	**50**
Middlesbrough	38	13	10	15	48	44	49
Charlton Athletic	38	14	7	17	45	56	49
Birmingham City	38	13	9	16	41	49	48
Fulham	38	13	9	16	41	50	48
Leeds United	38	14	5	19	58	57	47
Aston Villa	38	12	9	17	42	47	45
Bolton Wanderers	38	10	14	14	41	51	44
West Ham United	38	10	12	16	42	59	42
West Bromwich Albion	38	6	8	24	29	65	26
Sunderland	38	4	7	27	21	65	19

Season 2003/2004

F.A. PREMIERSHIP

Arsenal	38	26	12	0	73	26	90
Chelsea	38	24	7	7	67	30	79
Manchester United	38	23	6	9	64	35	75
Liverpool	38	16	12	10	55	37	60
Newcastle United	38	13	17	8	52	40	56
Aston Villa	38	15	11	12	48	44	56
Charlton Athletic	38	14	11	13	51	51	53
Bolton Wanderers	38	14	11	13	48	56	53
Fulham	38	14	10	14	52	46	52
Birmingham City	38	12	14	12	43	48	50
Middlesbrough	38	13	9	16	44	52	48
Southampton	38	12	11	15	44	45	47
Portsmouth	38	12	9	17	47	54	45
Tottenham Hotspur	**38**	**13**	**6**	**19**	**47**	**57**	**45**
Blackburn Rovers	38	12	8	18	51	59	44
Manchester City	38	9	14	15	55	54	41
Everton	38	9	12	17	45	57	39
Leicester City	38	6	15	17	48	65	33
Leeds United	38	8	9	21	40	79	33
Wolverhampton Wanderers	38	7	12	19	38	77	33

Supporters' Guides & Other Titles

This top-selling series has been published annually since 1982 and contains 2003/2004 Season's results and tables, Directions, Photographs, Phone numbers, Parking information, Admission details, Disabled information and much more.

THE SUPPORTERS' GUIDE TO PREMIER & FOOTBALL LEAGUE CLUBS 2005

The 21st edition featuring all Premiership and Football League clubs. *Price £6.99*

THE SUPPORTERS' GUIDE TO NON-LEAGUE FOOTBALL 2005 – STEP 1 & STEP 2 CLUBS

Following the reorganisation of Non-League Football this 13th edition covers all 66 Step 1 & Step 2 clubs – effectively the Football Conference and it's feeder Leagues. *Price £6.99*

THE SUPPORTERS' GUIDE TO NON-LEAGUE FOOTBALL 2005 – STEP 3 CLUBS

Following the reorganisation of Non-League Football the 1st edition of this book features all 66 clubs which feed into the Football Conference. *Price £6.99*

THE SUPPORTERS' GUIDE TO SCOTTISH FOOTBALL 2005

The 13th edition featuring all Scottish Premier League, Scottish League and Highland League clubs. *Price £6.99*

THE SUPPORTERS' GUIDE TO WELSH FOOTBALL GROUNDS 2005

The 9th edition featuring all League of Wales, Cymru Alliance & Welsh Football League Clubs + results, tables & much more. *Price £6.99*

FOOTBALL LEAGUE TABLES 1888-2004

The 7th edition contains every Football League, Premier League, Scottish League and Scottish Premier League Final Table from 1888-2004 together with Cup Final Information. *Price £9.99*

NON-LEAGUE FOOTBALL TABLES 1889-2004

The 3rd edition contains final tables for the Conference, it's 3 feeder Leagues and 4 Northern Leagues in England (which were not included in previous editions). *Price £9.95*

These books are available UK & Surface post free from –

Soccer Books Limited (Dept. SBL)
72 St. Peter's Avenue
Cleethorpes
N.E. Lincolnshire
DN35 8HU